## *About the cover...*

The striking juxtaposition of the title of the book and the honest and frank images detailed in this remarkable portrait captures the essence of authenticity and genuine experiences, the first steps of our profound journey reliving moments from childhood to adulthood.

This arresting, truthful picture beautifully contrasts the old-world respect for ceremony (note the father in shirt and tie, mother's hair carefully combed, she adorned with earrings) with the Americanization of the children for whom under-shirts are dress enough. The crowded table references a close-knit community where bonds are shared among friends, family, and potential tesori. In this rich neighborhood culture, people look out for one another, bridging the gap between generations.

The book cover portrays the raw and unfiltered realities of life for immigrants. We note the absence of lobster and Prime Rib. We also note the table full of good food. No Chateau Petrus,1966? Plenty of table wine. And didn't each of us eat off of one of those aluminum-framed Formica tables?

The choice of vernacular beauty over Disney-style Pollyanna for the cover invite us to open the book to enjoy a collection of unadorned illustrations and stories presenting the Italo life-style, unvarnished and immediate. And pure magic.

# Do You Believe in Magic?
*Anthology of Stories from the North End*

Edited by Dom Capossela

Publisher: Victor Passacantilli and Dom Capossela

Copyright ownership: Victor Passacantilli and Dom Capossela

Publication date: 2023

ISBN: 9781088062029

Captions for the photographs were written by Dom Capossela.

All profits from the sale of this book will go to charities in Boston's North End.

Dom can be reached at domcapossela@hotmail.com

Victor can be reached at victorbls1961@gmail.com

Dedicated to Dr. Mike (Mike Annunziata) and all of our other friends who are not here to share this moment with us.

# Acknowledgements

Each author's contribution to the anthology adds to the rich tapestry of our Italian neighborhood, weaving vivid illustrations of our shared experiences from sixty years ago, when we were just kids. Through their unique voices, these thirty authors capture our childhood, preserving its cherished memories for generations to come.

Vito Aluia, not a writer, but the generously sharing professional collector of North End photographs.

Vince Amicangelo writes about grade schoolers dressed as monks and parading through the streets.

Anthony 'Tony' Antidormi shares several noteworthy experiences.

Johanne Brogna writes the perfect capsule re: mama.

Dom Capossela has several entries, a couple of them lengthy, that, when combined, make him a robust contributor.

Anthony Cintolo, whose five childhood impressions add greatly to understanding the magic.

Anthony Coppola declares to anyone pleading ignorance, "You're Supposed to Know."

Anthony Cortese writes lovingly about a religious store his family operated.

Nick Dello Russo, shares the experience of growing up in the middle of the Haymarket and his reflections on the religious stores of the North End.

Nick DiMasi writes three pieces, all contributing to the picture of the North End.

Howard Dinin brings the perspective of an outsider who recognizes the magic, but is too distracted to participate.

Ron Fuccillo lives life as the model North Ender, illustrating responsibilities to family, duty, and honor.

Alex Goldfeld writes as an outsider fitting in.

Lisa Pasto Gurney writes admiringly about North End mothers.

Lucille Bova Guzzone submits a unique entry.

Frankie Imbergamo, a local celebrity, shares a recipe and technique.

Ralph Indrisano, a bit off the beaten track, shows that differences will always reveal themselves.

Arthur Laurentano adds a family portrait to the experiences.

Victor Passacantilli contributes several articles to the anthology, including a piece on the iconic Blue Front restaurant.

Jim Pasto's unique way of looking at things shows up in his insightful Foreword.

Steve Paterna asks, "Doesn't everybody know who we were?"

Diane Pesaturo, one of four female contributors, (Yes, we did solicit the girls,) presents her thoughts in an intriguing style.

Gus Pesaturo, in a single piece, gives us several insights into the North End.

Ron Polcari, aka Ron Robin, aka the man who introduced rock and roll into the North End (when 'Gee' hit the charts), tells a comical piece about the Holy Eucharist. Hope God has a sense of humor.

Joe Sarno talks about two friends who meant a great deal to him.

Lino Viola shares several entries treating with completely different topics.

Sammy Viscione, at eleven entries, takes the title of most prolific of the contributors.

And to the friends and advisors who shared their counsel and technical skill: Howard Dinin, Tucker Johnson, and Jim Pasto.

And to the staff at FONE, keenly aware of where profits from the sale of this book should be directed.

# Epigraph

When does the past become the past?
How much time must elapse before what merely happened be-
gins to give off the mysterious numinous glow that is the mark
of true pastness?

After all, the resplendent vision we carry with us in memory
was once merely the present, dull and workaday and wholly
unremarkable, except in those moments when one has just
fallen in love, say, or won the lottery, or has been delivered bad
news by the doctor.

What is the magic that is worked upon experience, when it is
consigned to the laboratory of the past, there to be shaped and
burnished to a finished radiance?

Certain moments in certain places, apparently insignificant,
imprint themselves on the memory with improbable vividness
and clarity – improbable because, so clear & vivid are they, the
suspicion arises that one's fancy must have made them up: that
one must, in a word, have imagined them.

Let us say, the present is where we live, while the past is where
we dream. Yet if it is a dream, it is substantial and sustaining.
The past buoys us up, a tethered & ever-expanding hot-air bal-
loon. And yet, I ask again, what is it? What transmutation must
the present go through in order to become the past? Time's
alchemy works in a bright abyss.

**—John Banville, "Time Pieces"**

### Lou Monte, "Lazy Mary"

"Lazy Mary you better get up"

She answered back, "I am not able"

"Lazy Mary you better get up

We need the sheets for the table"

"Lazy Mary you smoke in bed

There's only one man you should marry

My advice to you would be

Is to pay attention to me"

"You better marry a fireman he'll come and go,

Go and come
*"Sempr's la pompa a mano tiene."*
(Always with his hose in his hand.)

**Louie Prima, "What Did George Washington say?"**
"Give me liberty or give me death"—these words will never die.

"We have just begun to fight" is a famous battle cry;

But what I really want to know ain't written anywhere.

Hey, what did Washington say when he crossed the Delaware?

"On the day of glory, that's what Georgie told his crew.

Some may doubt the story, but to those of you who do,

Just ask Giusepp' the barber while he trims and cuts your hair.

He'll tell you just what Georgie said when he crossed the Delaware:

... *Ho freddo e non indosso biancheria intima*
(I'm hungry, I'm cold, and I don't have any underwear,)
or, the North End translation,
(I'm hungry, I'm cold, and my balls are freezing.)


Oh, Martha, Martha, no pasta fazool tonight.

Oh, Martha, Martha, I'm not coming home tonight."

## Louie Prima, "Luigi."

There's a fella named Luigi
He comes from Italy
I wanna be like Luigi 'cause he's always got money
With a book in his pocket, a pencil in his hand
Luigi's got-a the bees-a-knees that I no understand
He stand-a on the corner, I think-a he waste his time
People come up to him and say "Number five-a for-a dime"
Hey Luigi, Whadda you do?
Hey Luigi teach-a me too
When you come here, you no can count
Now you make-a the money by the big amount

With Luigi things are cookin' he dress-a like a duke
He's-a no what you call good lookin' but he sure is a lookin' good
"Hello Hello Luigi" The pretty girls all say he's no Giovan Amici, but still
he's a do okay
On every one of the fingers, he flash-a the big-a jewel
Now he can buy the caviar, he's through with pasta fazool
Hey Luigi whadda you do?
Hey Luigi teach-a me too
When you come here, you big-a bum, now you make-a the money by the
big-a sum

Now a funny thing-a happen, it happened yesterday
The police-a-man he come and take Luigi far away
Goodbye, goodbye Luigi, I no like to see you go
I know just how you feeling, but I make-a the dough
Don't you worry Luigi, I call-a you on the phone, I'll take over the numbers
while you crack-a the big stone
Hey Luigi! I'm-a no fool
Hey Luigi! Ah you're a chidrool*
I take-a the numbers, but not like you think
I'm-a the policeman who put you in the clink
My dear paisanos, I'm telling you, don't be like Luigi or the police-a-man
will get you too"

*The word "chidrool" is a dialectal version of the Italian word "centriolo"
which means cucumber. It is used as a slang term in some regions of Italy to
refer to someone who is foolish or stupid.

# Contents

## Restaurants, Luncheonettes, and other Food Shops in the 1950s-60s North End

### Vignettes

# Foreword
## by Jim Pasto

As you read the collection of stories that Dom and Victor have gathered, keep in mind that while the stories are now words written on a page, they had two lives before they got there. The first life was that of a 'life lived' in the sense that they were things that actually happened. They began as events, as experiences. The second life is that of a 'life told' in the sense that the original events were then recounted verbally to others; they were told as 'stories' of things that had actually happened. In the process, this 'reincarnation' of the events as stories became new events themselves as the stories were passed along, told and retold again, making themselves part of the everyday fabric of life as we knew it in the North End. The North End was a world of happenings and stories of happenings. It was a collective life of people and their stories.

The stories that follow are a collection from this collective life, making them a third life, a 'life read' as words on these pages. You can read them aloud with and to others, you can read them on your own. Most likely you will read them on your own, quietly, maybe even reflectively, with a sense of nostalgia, a sense of reading about a collective life that has just about passed away and so has to be preserved in a book like this, for us to read and also for us to pass on to others who did not experience that life or did not hear these stories told on the streets or the clubs and apartments of the North End. Therefore, while the gathering of these stories is a sign that the life we once lived is "all over," keep in mind too that the gathering of this book is an event itself and story itself, so that really story goes on with this book. If you make it so. If when you share it with others, you do so as a story that in its telling becomes a new event. A new story. The North End story

I don't mean to make it sound complicated. It is just that I do feel a mix of sadness and happiness in writing this. Our old life in the North End is just about passed away. The North End is still there, and the people there still experience it and talk about it in their own way, making it fast becoming "their" story and no longer "our story." That is okay. At least they will know our story from our stories in this book.

These stories are not the whole story, and they are not by any means all the stories that were told of the life we lived in the North End. That would take many books. These stories are a sample. A sample of stories and so a sample of that life we lived in the North End. Enjoy them. Pass them along. Keep them alive.


Love,


Jim

# Preface

I publish a weekly magazine: existentialautotrip. While thinking about content for upcoming issues, I thought an article on the North End would be rich. Then, I thought, not just any article, but a cover story; then, no, an entire issue.

I pushed away from my screen, rose up, and paced. None of the above, actually. The Italian North End needs its own book – our childhood was special. As I paced, I asked myself, seriously, Why? Everybody has a childhood. Why the North End, especially?

Here's what I answered. Most people we know remember their childhood fondly, ready, at the drop of a hat, to relate stories of the good old days. But there is something in the childhood memories of us old time North Enders that is so passionate that the passion is its own separate story. But why, I asked myself, are we so passionate?

Thus, the conception: a story that answers to that Why?

Do you believe in magic? Because we'll tell you about magic that'll make you feel groovy, make you feel happy like an old-time movie. So suspend your disbelief because, if you do, you'll get the 'why so,' as in 'passionate.'

We begin by setting the scene: a Prologue to put us in era, era starting in the 1950s. Scene set, we pull in memories, in the event, those of thirty writers recounting more than fifty stories and observations, all evidencing the magic. We end with an Epilogue summarizing our roles in that era, what we took and what we returned, in spades.

Enjoy the reading, my friends, as we, from the 1950s Italian North End, enjoy the telling. We will make you believe in, as we believe in: magic.

# Prologue
## By Dom Capossela

Do you believe in magic?

If you do, come. If you don't, give us a moment to change your attitude. Please, everyone, take two steps forward, so you are all fully on the carpet. Sit, please. We want you to be comfortable while we prepare the backdrop against which our writers can post memories that were unique to the North End. This is a collection of stories about that magical place, beloved by hundreds of thousands, perhaps millions, of visitors, and tens of thousands of Italos brought up there. Italo, in this Prologue, refers to American-born, American citizens of Italian heritage. Italo: easier and more accurate to say than "Italian-American."

We're floating back to the 1950s. Let's begin with a review of the energy pulsating through the entire nation. Oops! Hold your knees for balance. That's it. Hang on. We're landing.

We had just elected a new President, the Republican, Dwight D. Eisenhower. Look at his face: he's daddy. Calm. An easy chair and pipe kind of guy. After leading us through the Second World War, he will soon help to end the Korean War, and give America a decade of rest and recreation. That's what voters believed when they elected him, and that's what they wanted.

*A father figure who calmed us while our world was being rocked*

*Were we happy the war was over?*

19

# DeAmato Family Army Veterans

<<<<<<<<<

**Ralph DeAmato,** the son of Giovanni and Ascenza D'Amato, was 20 years old when drafted in 1943, and had a ranking of Staff Sargeant. He was in a Combat Infantry Unit that fought in World War II in Europe. He was wounded during the war and received the Purple Heart. Bronze Star and the Combat Infantry Badge.

>>>>>>>>>>>>

**Pat DeAmato,** son of Giovanni and Ascenza D'Amato, was 22 years old when drafted in 1951, rank was PFC (private first class ) and he served during the Korean War. He was stationed in Germany as a Combat Infantry during the war. In 1952, he took leave to meet his mother who had traveled to Italy visit her mother and son Fr. Norbert, who was studying in Rome.

Ralph 1943 - 1945

Pat 1951 - 1953

<<<<<<<<<<

**Frank DeAmato,** son of Giovanni and Ascenza D'Amato, was 20 years old when drafted in 1953, his rank was a Corporal and he served during the Korean War. He was stationed at Camp Polk, Louisana and Fort Riley, Kansas during the War.

>>>>>>>>>>>>

**John (D.A.) DeAmato,** son of Giovanni and Ascenza D'Amato, was 23 years old when drafted in 1959, his rank was a Spec. 4, ( Specialist Fourth Class or Corporal ). He served during the Berlin Crisis of (1961) as a Security Gate Guard at Tague, South Korea.

Frank 1953 - 1955

John (D.A.) 1959 - 1961

<<<<<<<<<<<<<<<<<<

**John De Amato,** son of Carmen and Edith DeAmato, joined the Army Reserves in 1963 for six years and attained the rank of E-6 ( Staff Sargeant ). He was ready for active duty at any time if his unit was called in time of crisis. Fortunately his unit was not called to active duty

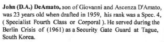
>>>>>>>>>>>>>

**Clifford Walton - DeAmato,** son of John ( D.A. ) and Kathy Walton - DeAmato, he was 20 years old when he joined the Army on February 12, 2003. 15 months after the bombing of the Twin Towers on 9-11-01. When the Iraq War started on March 2003 his training was cut short. Stationed in Iraq during the war, repairing tanks and heavy equipment and was awarded the "National Defense Service Medal, Global War on Terrorism Service Medal, Army Service Ribbon.

John (Anthony) 1965 - 1971

Clifford 2003 - 2006

*The DeAmato family. Our own version of the five Sullivan brothers who inspired a movie called "The Fighting Sullivans."*

*Stephen Joseph Steriti killed in action in Vietnam*
*May 8th 1966. Posthumously awarded the Silver*
*Star on June 1st 1966. Domenic Piso, photo*

*Despite the hot war being over, a Cold War had begun. Russia had "the bomb"*
*and we school children learned to duck under our desks in case one of them*
*exploded nearby.*

After all, during these destructive wars, our little North End community sacrificed as much as any.

Adult society wanted peace and relaxation. It's not what they got. Thank Goodness! We kids wanted something else. We must have wished harder.

Do you remember, "Who knows what evil lurks in the hearts of men?" You don't. It's not your fault you're too young. That question was from the introduction of a radio drama, the words eerily spoken by the show's narrator, Lamont Cranston, at the beginning of each episode. "The Shadow" was a popular radio show that aired from 1937 to 1954, featuring a mysterious crime-fighting vigilante who became a cultural icon. Like the others across America, we North End kids gathered around our radios to listen to that and other of our favorite radio programs. But that was the world before television.

The first television was a bulky console with limited channels, an external antenna, a black-and-white display, and manual controls.

The TV set took center stage in living rooms, although not many of us North Enders had dedicated living rooms. Instead, most TVs were in our parents' bedrooms, which were larger

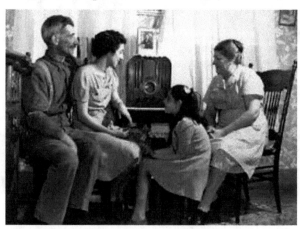

*The magic of the transition from radio to television touched us. No one ever wanted to go back.*

*Most television sets were basic. Setting the screen in a beautiful piece of furniture was not only expensive but took up a lot more room.*

than the other rooms. We would sporadically tune in to the often feeble programming, usually at times between 7.00pm to 11.00pm when the programs were broadcast. Our viewing time was extended, however, in 1954, when Steve Allen hosted the inaugural episode of 'The Tonight Show,' which premiered on NBC on September 27. That show ran until 1.00am and set the foundation for the late-night talk show format that continues to this day.

Despite the tiny screens, despite the black and white format, TV's impact on America's youth, including us North Enders, was enormous. It changed the way we dressed, the way we bought things, the heroes we chose to emulate, our standards of right and wrong, and more, much more. For example, American Bandstand, at its 1952 inception an all-white show, did a 180 when, in 1956, Dick Clark assumed the role of host. He featured music by black artists, had black artists perform on the show, and integrated the regulars who danced on the show. This iconic program featured exclusively rock and roll music, and, not only taught us how to dance to it, but also taught black and white teenagers it's alright to hang together. American Bandstand became a cultural touchstone, reflecting the evolving spirit of the nation. AB helped our tightly-knit, insular neighborhood get a view of the larger world outside.

Although truly magical, television was not all sunshine and roses for the North End. While we did enjoy the entertainment that television provided, we were also sensitive to the reality that much of the programming was inimical to how Italos were perceived by middle-America. An example.

In April 1951, the Kefauver Army Hearings (Officially, the "Senate Special Committee to Investigate Crime in Interstate Commerce.") was broadcast. Estes Kefauver, the good Senator from Tennessee, the chair of the committee, held America's viewing audience in thrall with televised hearings held to discover organized crime's connection to interstate commerce. Day after day, he brought suspects forward to grill them about their involvement.

Day after day, the roll was called: "Joseph Bonanno," "Joe Valachi," "Frank Costello." The preponderance of Italo names led Middle America, most of whom had not either visited the North End or personally known any Italos, to conclude that most criminals were Italos, and most Italos were criminals. What else could they think? They saw it on television.

Secure in our Italo enclave, we didn't let prejudices affect how we behaved. But it hurt. In the North End, among ourselves, we shared many stories of parents refusing to let their children go out on dates with us. We were bad guys (or girls). They saw it on television.

Secure in our Italo enclave, who cared what they thought. Really. But it hurt.

Yes, TV was magical. In the North End we appreciated Lucille Ball and Milton Berle, laughed at Sid Caesar and Jackie Gleason, and respected Bishop Sheen. We watched "Father Knows Best" and "Ozzie and Harriet" even though all of the family

*Frank Costello, American mobster, testifying before the Kefauver*
*Committee investigating organized crime*
*Al Aumuller, World Telegram staff photographer - Library of*
*Congress. New York World-Telegram & Sun Collection.*
*These were scary guys. Criminals or citizens, they elicited re-*
*spect. We admired them for that.*
*But scary.*
*Captured so well in Joe Pesci's classic scene with Ray Liotta in*
*"Goodfellas." Remember? Everyone is laughing and joking until*
*Liotta's character, Henry Hill, says to Tommy, "You're a funny*
*guy."*
*Suddenly a chill descends on the entire gang, fifty strong, and*
*silence rules.*
*Joe Pesci's character, Tommy DeVito, says, "Funny how? I mean,*
*funny like I'm a clown? I amuse you?"*
*This memorable quote precipitates a tense and unsettling conver-*
*sation during which the immediate murder of good friend Henry*
*Hill suddenly becomes a distinct possibility.*
*Scary guys, as seen through the brilliance of Martin Scorsese*
*storytelling.*
*Did I forget to mention how that moment ends?*
*Watch the movie, dummkopf.*

series were non-ethnic, white, and middle-class, untouched by serious arguments, illnesses, crime, or divorce. But while we watched, we didn't recognize these people. The lives they portrayed were light years distant from our own.

Early television did feature three Italo entertainers. Perry Como was first. His variety show, "The Chesterfield Supper Club," based on his successful radio program, made its television debut early in television history: 1950. Perry captivated audiences and paved the way for the incomparable, Frank Sinatra, whose show, "The Frank Sinatra Show," started in 1952.

Annette Funicello, an unknown, became the third Italo entertainer to emerge a star on early television. On December 22, 1955, she crash landed onto the national entertainment scene as a Mouseketeer in "The Mickey Mouse Club." Annette's charm and talent captivated audiences. She was, by popular acclaim,

*Publicity photo of American
entertainer Annette Funicello
(circa 1975).
Our Sweetheart*

the North End's communal heartthrob.

Her stardom was a lovely moment for us North Enders. Emphasis on 'moment', since it took ten years before another Italo broke through into television success. That was in 1965, when Dean Martin was chosen to host yet another variety show.

Television had been America's chief entertainment for twenty-five years before an Italo performer or character was featured in either a comedy or drama series. The drought ended in 1974, when Happy Days, produced by Garry Marshall, himself of an Italo father, introduced us to the much-loved Arthur Herbert Fonzarelli, "The Fonz."

Fonzy instantly became the poster boy for the greaser subculture: America's rebellious, working-class youth, with slicked-back hair, leather jacket, jeans, and motorcycle boots. He rode

*Publicity photo from Happy Days. Pictured*
*are Richie (Ron Howard) and Fonzie (Hen-*
*ry Winkler) at Fonzie's apartment over the*
*Cunningham's garage. The episode deals with*
*Fonzie's destroyed motorcycle.*

a motorcycle and was perceived as a tough and streetwise person, with a barely disguised disregard for authority. Despite that Henry Winkler who played him was Jewish, and despite that Fonzie was a caricature of Italo thuggery, we loved him as an Italo, him and his famous, "Aaayyy."

As we also loved the Happy Days spinoff, Laverne and Shirley, the draw being the show's Italo costar, Laverne DeFazio. And who can forget John Travolta and his 'Vinnie Barbarino', a Fonzie clone.

*Travolta as Vinnie Barbarino in the*
*ABC comedy Welcome Back, Kotter,*
*c. 1976*
*John had quite the career.*

Notable: The greaser subculture was a spin-off from the motorcycle subculture dominated twenty years prior by Marlon Brando (The Wild One) and, his disciple, James Dean (Rebel without a Cause). Leather jackets, t-shirts, jeans, and resistance to authority were traits common to both groups. They were us. We ate it up.

Notable: The King, Elvis Presley, at times incorporated elements of the Wild One into his persona, often wearing black leather jackets, jeans, and boots. These outfits, along with his signature pompadour hairstyle, contributed to his rebellious image and helped establish him as a cultural icon associated with

*We were young and a little wild, i.e. listening to our friends and not our parents. We were sometimes insulting to Old Timers, calling them 'greasers', not meaning anything good by it. I think about who I was and I am ashamed and sorry for so many things that I did.*

rock and roll and youth rebellion.

Notable: As pre-teens, we often used 'greaser' in a pejorative way: to insult Italian immigrants, especial those old timers who spoke broken-English. We resented their attempts to foist Old World culture on us. We were struggling to define ourselves as Americans. We were nasty. Che peccato! Shame on us.

Television cast Italos only as clowns and crooners for its first three decades. It took thirty years before television deigned to present an intelligent, thoughtful, moral, competent Italo hero. Finally, in 1981, Captain Francis X. Furillo, played by Daniel Travanti, appeared. His was a brilliant rendering of a police chief. We were ecstatic. The series was highly successful.

Notable. Despite that we were a working-class neighborhood, we afforded TV sets pretty early after their introduction, an

*"Pizza man," his girlfriend called him. She had the right. Loving him gave her the right. He was an Italo character we could relate to; be proud of. Unless, of course, you were one of the very, very few Italos who were member of oc (organized crime).*

indication that our parents and families were becoming more prosperous. The Beatles weren't the only ones singing, "Got to admit it's getting better."

Notable. Television, in 2023, remains significantly openly anti-Italo. Stereotypical portrayals of Italos as criminals or thugs still abound. It pisses me off more and more, thinking that the writers and producers of the shows that do that, for example, Blacklist, know better. You think I exaggerate? I asked Chat GPT this question: Why does the TV show Blacklist portray so many criminals as being Italian? AI's answer is anything but a denial: "The TV show "Blacklist" does portray some criminals as being Italian or having Italian connections. However, it is important to note that the show's portrayal of criminals does not reflect the entire Italian community or imply that being Italian inherently makes someone a criminal." Ha! An exemplar of damning with faint praise. Assholes.

Notable: The American TV series called Suits was playing in the background as I typed these pages, on June 24, 2023. Among the hundreds of characters that come and go or get talked about on the show, few ever have an Italian surname. Tonight there was one (whom we never see): Rimini, his name. He was described several times, always negatively, with two references to his dirty shoes. No big thing, right? He's a minor character; not even a character. But honestly, after several hundred thousand such references over the years, I want to shake a writer or a producer by the lapels and say, "Come on! What's the matter with you? What the fuck is the matter with you?"

Notable: For us teenagers in the 50s, 60s, and 70s, although we watched television, watched what other people thought of us, our entire ethnic generation was following the yellow brick road for future success. While our immigrant parents were happy just to have a job, we pushed ourselves forward, enrolling in colleges, learning trades, starting small businesses.

So, television and the American middle-class either stereotyped us as criminals or ignored us as not being talented? Well, we ignored them in return, and made something of ourselves. And our ultimate payback to these haters, many of us married their

31

children.

If television were the only magic moment of the era, we would still consider this era as magical. But another, equally impactful revolution, took place during the same years as the emergence of television. And just as television replaced radio as America's main source of entertainment, we teens, although having been raised on Swing and Big Band, Jazz, and Traditional Pop, (the Frank Sinatra, Nat 'King' Cole music), replaced all of our parents' popular music with a fusion of rhythm and blues, gospel, and country music that we called rock and roll.

*Chuck Berry's lyrics touched us where we lived:*

*Sweet Little Sixteen*
*Oh mommy, mommy*
*Please may I go*
*It's such a sight to see*
*Somebody steal the show*

*Johnny B Goode*
*Deep down in Louisiana, close to New Orleans*
*Way back up in the woods among the evergreens*
*There stood a log cabin made of earth and wood*
*Where lived a country boy named Johnny B. Goode*
*Who never ever learned to read or write so well*
*But he could play the guitar just a-ringin' a bell.*
*Go! Go!*

Our parents heard the first songs and exclaimed, Omigod! This music is crazy loud. These voices are caterwauls. The sexual lyrics, suggestive performances, and way-too-intimate dancing will lead to promiscuity, they said. They also remonstrated, many of the stars are black, so, there go the racial barriers and cultural boundaries that have kept our country happily segregated and culturally pure. On top of all that, they yakked, rock and roll is creating a generation gap between our children and ourselves that didn't exist before.

*Ms Francis had a huge hit in 1958 when her "Who's Sorry Now" went to #4 on the Billboard charts.*

*Photo of Dion and The Belmonts from the magazine Hit Parader*
*from September 1960.*
*The Belmonts were an American vocal trio prominent through-*
*out the 1950s. All of its members were from the Bronx, New York*
*City. In 1957, Dion DiMucci joined them and the established*
*trio of Angelo D'Aleo, Carlo Mastrangelo and Fred Milano*
*formed a quartet with DiMucci. One of the group was serving in*
*the Navy when the picture was taken.*

They were so right. On all counts. Rock and roll celebrated
teenaged rebellion and freedom of expression. Loud? We wanted it louder. Maybe not promiscuity, but rock and roll definitely
led to a reexamination of sexual mores. Black stars? Of course:
they had a major hand in creating and popularizing the music.
And a generation gap? Wrong: chasm more like it.

Notable: African American artists like Chuck Berry, Fats Dom-
ino, and Little Richard won us teenagers over. They did more

*Starting as a teen idol in the late 1950s, he achieved chart success with hits like "Splish Splash" and "Dream Lover." Darin then transitioned into a more sophisticated sound, exploring jazz, swing, and adult contemporary music. He recorded the timeless classic "Mack the Knife," which won him two Grammy Awards.*

*Beyond his singing career, Darin ventured into acting and appeared in films and television shows. His versatility, charisma, and dynamic stage presence captivated audiences. Darin died at thirty-seven years old.*

*Darin actively supported Bobby Kennedy's bid for the Democratic nomination for President and was at the Ambassador Hotel when Bobby Kennedy was assassinated there.*

to bridge racial divides than Malcolm X, Thurgood Marshall, and Martin Luther King, Jr. ever did.

From its inception, rock and roll music was big in the North End. Being inner city kids, we were immediately drawn to other inner-city kids, to the black-oriented or independent radio stations that featured the new music, only returning to main-stream stations after they adopted rock and roll formats. Rock music ruled. At times, the new hit songs, the new artists, were all we talked about.

Unlike television, rock and roll took very kindly to Italo per-formers. Connie Francis, Annette Funicello, Fabian, Frankie Avalon, Bobby Darin, Freddy Bell, Dion, and Johnny Maestro were only some of the Italo rock and roll stars of the 1950s.

Notable: North End rumors had it that the Philadelphia Mafia had a hand in guiding the careers of several of these. Good luck to them, was the North End attitude.

There were bits of bases for the rumors. It's true, for example, that Bobby Darin's maternal grandfather, Saverio Antonio, "Big Sam Curly" Cassotto, (born January 26, 1882), who was of Italian descent and who died in prison from pneumonia a year before Darin's birth, was a made man, a "soldier" in the Genovese Crime Family, and a close associate of Frank Costello.

We discussed these things but passed no judgment.

While we were pleased that so many Italos made it to the top, the North End had our own talented singing groups and some of us were bothered that no one with juice ever stepped up to use their influence to help our own paesani carve out singing careers. Hey, "Quel sarà, sarà."

Notable: When Bob Dylan sang, "Times They Are a-Changin'" in 1964, people who didn't understand the magic of the 1950s thought Dylan was a prophet. But the truth is that the times were changing in 1954, a full ten years before Dylan made his announcement. Bob Dylan is a historian.

Notable: Consider that Dylan's 1964 audience was essentially college students in their early twenties. Ten years prior, 1954, those twenty-somethings were ages ten or older. Dylan's 1964 fan base was us, reaping the fruit of changing times born from the seeds we planted a decade ago.

More pixie dust that made the age profound: the transistor. This semiconductor device made it possible to create smaller portable radios that allowed us young teenagers to listen to music outside of our homes. I remember our gang dancing at 10.00pm to the music from the first transistor radios. It was a hoot: another reason for us to go home later than our parents were demanding. Transistor radios allowed us to listen to our anthemic music while hanging on the corner. We were already bonded but those late teenaged nights in the playground were transcendent.

*A classic Emerson transistor radio, circa 1958*
*Joe Haupt from USA - Emerson Model 888 Pioneer 8-Transistor AM Radio, Made in the USA, Circa 1958*
*Emerson Model 888 Pioneer 8-Transistor AM Radio, Made in the USA, Circa 1958*

*An old rotary dial telephone. Compared to our cell phone, it didn't do much, but it did permit us to conduct a conversation when we were too far apart to be heard directly.*

Another magic moment was the introduction of the telephone. No, not the device that sends and receives texts, takes photos and videos, browses the internet, downloads apps and games, listens to music, watches videos, uses GPS navigation, sends and receives emails, uses social media apps like Facebook, Twitter, and Instagram, makes mobile payments, or becomes a flashlight. A telephone.

You want to talk to your buddy across the street. You head for the window to shout out his name, and then you stop. You have a telephone. You walk to the phone and pick up the headset, you dial the number that you wrote on the wall and wait. He finally picks up and you say, "So, what are you gonna do tonight, Marty?" You want to check up on your grandmother? Arrange dates? Call an ambulance? The telephone. We all raced to get on the list to have one installed.

"What are you rebelling against?"

" Whaddyagot?"

*One of the greatest actors in American history in one of his early great movies.*

This iconic line, spoken by motorcycle group leader, Johnny Strabler, portrayed by Marlon Brando, in the 1953 film, "The Wild One," was idiomatic of the transformation of Hollywood's portrayal of heroes and heroines. Johnny Strabler was a rebellious biker who embodied a defiant and nonconformist attitude. When asked the question, his response expresses his rebellious nature and indifference to societal norms. In the North End, we were tough guys: defiant and having our own set of morals. To prove it, we adopted the motorcycle dress. It fit how we saw ourselves.

Goodbye, John Wayne and Gary Cooper, the traditional archetypes known for their stoicism, bravery, and adherence to traditional values.

Hello, Marlon Brando and James Dean, and a new breed of actors who brought a fresh approach to the concept of heroism. Hello, to more nuanced and psychologically rich characters, characters that had a lasting impact on cinema and future generations of performers.

*Hepburn in a screen test for Roman*
*Holiday (1953) which was also used as*
*promotional material for the film*

Brando and Dean introduced a sense of vulnerability, complexity, and introspection to their characters, reflecting the changing social and cultural landscape of the time. These actors embraced a more naturalistic acting style, focusing on raw emotions and authenticity. They were closer to reflecting our own personalities.

Brando's performances, particularly in films like "A Streetcar Named Desire" (1951) and "On the Waterfront" (1954), adopting the method acting approach, brought a level of intensity and psychological depth previously unseen on screen.

James Dean, with his roles in "Rebel Without a Cause" (1955) and "East of Eden" (1955), portrayed characters who were disillusioned and conflicted, challenging social norms and embodying a sense of alienation that resonated with us.

Montgomery Clift brought a depth of emotion and vulnerability to his characters. Films like "A Place in the Sun" (1951) and "From Here to Eternity" (1953) showcased his ability to convey complex inner struggles.

*Theatrical release poster for the 1955 film Blackboard Jungle.
"Copyright 1955 Loew's Incorporated" - Scan via Heritage Auctions. Cropped from original image and retouched by uploader; see unretouched version in upload history.*
*Blackboard Jungle is a 1955 American social drama film about an
English teacher in an interracial inner-city school, based on the
1954 novel The Blackboard Jungle by Evan Hunter and adapted
for the screen and directed by Richard Brooks. It is remembered
for its innovative use of rock and roll in its soundtrack, for casting
grown adults as high school teens, and for the unique breakout role
of a black cast member, film icon Sidney Poitier, as a rebellious yet
musically talented student.*

Paul Newman, with his striking looks and magnetic screen presence, tackled morally ambiguous characters in films like "Cat on a Hot Tin Roof" (1958) and "Cool Hand Luke" (1967). He infused depth and complexity into his performances.

These men were our new heroes. Of course, the new wave affected actresses, too.

Elizabeth Taylor demonstrated her range and depth as an actress in films like "A Place in the Sun" (1951) and "Cat on a Hot Tin Roof" (1958). She delved into characters dealing with personal conflicts and emotional turmoil.

Audrey Hepburn ventured into complex roles in films like "Roman Holiday" (1953) and "Breakfast at Tiffany's" (1961). She portrayed characters dealing with identity crises and a longing for genuine connections.

On a more mundane level, a raft of teenaged movies were released in the 1950s that featured the new music and new values. We watched: Blackboard Jungle, Rock Around the Clock, High School Confidential, Summer Place, The Delinquents, Rock Around the Clock, Don't Knock the Rock, Jamboree!, The Girl Can't Help It, Rock, Rock, Rock!, Let's Rock, Rockabilly Baby, Shake, Rattle & Rock!, Hot Rod Girl, and The Big Beat. Whew! Where did we find the time?

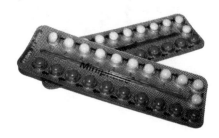

*It didn't need another name. The Pill says it all, as in, "Are you on the pill?"*

The Sexual Revolution which had a profound impact on sex and gender attitudes, although, perhaps, less on us growing up, as we did, under the auspices of the Catholic Church and old-school parents.

In 1948, Margaret Sanger helped found the International Committee on Planned Parenthood, which evolved into the International Planned Parenthood Federation in 1952, and soon became the world's largest non-governmental international women's health, family planning and birth control organization.

In the early 1950s, Sanger encouraged philanthropist Katharine McCormick to provide funding for biologist Gregory Pincus to develop the birth control pill which was eventually sold under the name Enovid.

In 1953, Playboy, an American men's lifestyle and entertainment magazine, hit the newsstands and was credited with an important role in the sexual revolution.

In 1957, Betty Friedan was asked to conduct a survey of her

*Known for its centerfolds of nude and semi-nude models (Playmates), Playboy played an important role in the sexual revolution.*

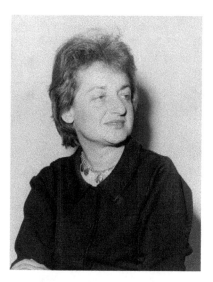

*American feminist and writer.
Fred Palumbo, World Telegram staff
photographer. Restored by Adam Cu-
erden - Library of Congress. New York
World-Telegram & Sun Collection.
Her 1963 book The Feminine Mystique is
often credited with sparking the second
wave of American feminism in the 20th
century.*

former Smith College classmates for their 15th anniversary reunion. She found that many of them were unhappy with their lives as housewives. That research prompted her to begin work on The Feminine Mystique, a book that is widely credited with sparking the beginning of feminism in the United States.

Three other events wrought major changes in American society.

In 1953, Earl Warren became Chief Justice of the Supreme Court. Two of his Court's most impactful rulings were Brown v Board of Education, a historic Supreme Court case that on May 17, 1954, held that segregation in public schools based on race was unconstitutional, so, advancing civil rights and promoting equality in education; and the second ruling, Miranda v Arizona which ruled that police must inform prisoners of their rights

*When the Warren Court held that schools segregated on the basis of race could not be equal, many parts of Boston's white areas had violent demonstrations in protest. But not us in the North End. Buses of children of color arrived and left without incident.*
*It was a proud day for us.*

to remain silent and to have an attorney present during police interrogations. These decisions were powerful agents of social improvement.

The Beat Generation, emerging in the 1950s, was a home-grown, USA countercultural literary movement. Beat writers such as Jack Kerouac, Allen Ginsberg, and William S. Burroughs explored themes of rebellion, spirituality, sexuality, and the search for personal freedom. The Beats celebrated spontaneity, jazz, drugs, and non-traditional lifestyles. Their works, characterized by stream-of-consciousness writing, explored the human condition and criticized the materialistic culture of the time. The Beat Generation's influence extended beyond literature, impacting music and art, and inspiring subsequent generations of countercultural movements.

*Lawrence Ferlinghetti*
*Elsa Dorfman - Own work*
*At the Grolier Bookshop in Harvard Square in the 1960s, with Gordon Cairnie, the owner at the time.*
*There were still some beat cafes around in the early sixties in Boston and Cambridge. I was a college freshman feeling very intellectual for having a coffee while people were reciting poetry, getting paid by passing the hat.*

*Giorgio Cavallon, the artist, was born March 3, 1904, in Sorio, a hamlet of the municipality of Gambellara near Vicenza Italy and immigrated to the US in 1920, becoming a citizen in 1929.*
*By the end of the 1940, Cavallon connected to the early generation of New York School Abstract Expressionist artists whose artistic innovation by the 1950s had been recognized across the Atlantic, including Paris.*

Finally, and apropos of nothing, an art dealer, Leo Castelli in 1951 mounted an exhibition he called the "Ninth Street Show." The body of work, a new style painting called Abstract Expressionism, abruptly established the ascendancy of American art throughout the world. Magic, magic everywhere.

"Th-th-th-that's all, folks!"

47

# The Gravy
## *The Empress of the Kitchen*
### By Dom Capossela

When we called out to our neighbors to recount memories of our experiences together, Sunday Gravy was far and away the most popular topic. We include only four testimonials.

What made Sunday's Gravy so compelling?

In a blue-collar neighborhood, the weekdays were spent on the job. Dinners were delicious but we were tired, and an easy chair and television were beckoning. Saturdays were filled with errands which crowded out a holiday-grade meal. That left Sundays to host what evolved into the North End's universally observed, universally cherished dinner: what we called "The Gravy".

Sunday Gravy was a tradition that transcended generations, carrying the echoes of our immigrant ancestors who had lovingly passed down the recipes, techniques, and values of family and community. On Gravy days, the aromas of simmering pots of meat and tomatoes filled our homes and joined the aromas seeping from the other apartments in the building, together flowing out onto the sidewalks and into the streets. What an environment.

I believe that what spinach did for Popeye, what Holy Communion did for our souls, The Gravy did for our communal spirit. The Gravy, Sunday's magnum opus, was the physical manifestation of the magic that was the North End of that bygone era.

Do I believe in magic? Pass the meatballs.

*Tasting meatballs*

# The Eternal Question: Gravy or Sauce
## By James Pasto

My non-Italian wife used to smile when I used the word "gravy" for the 'tomato sauce' we put on our 'pasta.' She never called it gravy. She called it sauce.

About 10 years or so ago I went to a reading of the excellent book called *Gravy Wars*, by Lorraine Ranalli. It was about the eternal question: What do we call "it" - gravy or sauce? Lorraine wrote that the Italians of South Philly called it gravy and she thought this usage was unique to South Philly. When I told her that up here in the North End, we – at least some of us – also called it gravy, she was surprised, and pleasantly so because she had some allies in the fight.

After that I started asking around. Most everyone that I asked from the North End called it "gravy," by which is meant the tomato sauce that we have on our pasta (that is, on our "macaroni" – which is not that American stuff with all that cheese on it and no 'gravy'). Most people also knew the word "marinara" or "marinara sauce." This was a quick sauce, with no meat. But some people called this "gravy" too.

As I continued to ask, I found that a lot of Italians who came to the U.S. after the war did called it sauce (*salsa*, *ragu*, *sugo*) and not gravy. That made me think it was strictly an Italian American term. But then I found some post-WWII immigrants who said gravy, and some Italian Americans who only said sauce. So I don't know what to think now.

In America, the term "gravy" means the sauce used for meat, like "meatloaf gravy." In Italy they don't use the term "gravy" at all, and when they say *salsa*, or *ragu*, or *sugo*, they mean "sauce," meat or no meat. So it could be that the early Italian immigrants assumed that in America, any 'sauce' that went with or on meat was gravy, and so they called it "gravy." Or it could be that in Italy of the past they called it gravy but now call it sauce.

The truth, of course, lies in heaven – where all the food is Italian. Once we know what they call it there we will know what it really is – gravy or sauce. Of course, since North Enders don't go to heaven – what would we do there? – it will remain for us "the eternal question."

By the way, my wife makes a fantastic gravy!

*Buy the right cut, pound it flatter than the butcher did, season it, copiously, roll it, tie it, fry it, simmer it, savor it.*

## Sunday, My Most Favorite Day
### By Victor Passacantilli

Sunday was a special day for me as a young boy and adolescent. 9 o'clock mass at St, Stephens Church was a ritual. Neighborhood boys and girls my age would get ready for the day by dressing in their Sunday best clothes. Sport jacket and slacks to match, white crisply ironed shirt and tie were the uniform of the day for the boys. North Enders were notorious for their affection to sartorial splendor, especially on Sunday.

After mass, the magical Sunday began. The love of food,

friends and family enveloped the rest of the day. I was fortunate enough to live on a block where all my relatives resided. So, for me to make the rounds and show up at doorways was a easy journey. First a stop in my Aunt Delia's apartment to sample her Sunday Gravy by dipping a hard piece of Italian bread into an aromatic and bubbling gravy. Up a few flights and I arrived at Aunt Hilda's house to eat a slice of fried eggplant. In the adjoining building lived their mother, Amaranda, my grandmother. You never knew what to expect here. Sometimes I would find a cooked goat's head resting on a silver platter, ready to be picked at by her "comares and "compares". There was always something for me though like a stuffed artichoke or a stuffed pepper. Next door was my great aunt, Marcella. She would invariably have some homemade gnocchi, light as pillows, ready to be savored. A few steps down Hanover St., I would find my aunt, Jenny. Her fried eggplant was outstanding. On the same floor in 452 Hanover was my Sicilian grandmother, Anna, affectionately called "Mama Annutza." She made the best meatballs. Each one created with lots of love and lots of garlic; in each bite you would chew into a visible morsel of garlic. Her Gravy was an award winner. It was just her own style made with ingredients that had no measurements. On

*Resist this, I dare you.*

rare occasions she would add a bunch of finocchio (fennel). I am not sure if that was something Sicilian. I never asked and it tasted somewhat different but nothing compared to her Sunday creation. On the way out, I had to pass by my mother's friend, Angie's apartment and the door was usually open. If she heard or saw me, she would call out to me to come in. I never resisted. Her nephew, Joe, my friend was always there and we would share a piece of braciola. Yes, we shared it because it was a man's sized one. No braciolettine for us men! Angie didn't put a hardboiled egg in her braciola and that's why I liked hers the best. That was usually the last stop unless Mrs. Giardini on the next floor down heard me on the stairs. I normally did not stop there because I was saving some room for my mother's meal but she was one of the few cooks that would add a piece of lamb to her Sunday gravy recipe. It was an occasional treat for me.

At home my 5 brothers and father sat at the agitated dining room table. My mother always standing and serving. The macaroni was reddened with a Gravy ready to delight the senses. Just then the bustle began as hands started reaching across the table for a meatball, grated cheese, a piece of bread or red pepper. This epicurean indulgence/ritual is a solemn occasion for

*Really, now, nothing compares, nothing compares, nothing compares to you.*

53

North End Italians on this most special day!

Mangia bene, bevi bene, vivere bene


## Sunday Dinner in the North End
### By Arthur A. Laurentano


Growing up in the Italian North End of Boston consisted of many experiences, incidents and traditions. One could tell the day of the week it was by the meals our mothers cooked.

Sunday was the best and most rewarding culinary experience for most North End families because it was macaroni day. Back in the forties, fifties and sixties it was never "pasta" it was macaroni. The Gravy was put on the stove early in the morning. In our house it was not sauce but Gravy. By the time you were out of bed and getting ready for Sunday Mass the Gravy was already cooking. The aroma in the apartment was beyond belief,

Along with the cooking of Gravy was the frying of meatballs to be put in the Gravy. This added to the aroma and made it impossible to avoid getting into them before they were dropped into the Gravy to continue cooking. Back then you could not eat before Sunday Mass, especially if you intended to receive communion. Many of us committed sin by sneaking in the kitchen and stealing at least one fried meatball.

We could not wait for Mass to be completed so we could get back home for the feast. The Gravy would still be simmering on the stove which gave us the opportunity to dip a piece of fresh scali bread into it. I can taste it now.

The macaroni varied from Sunday to Sunday. It could be home-made ravioli, manicotti, gnocchi, or cavatelli although store bought macaroni was also used. Other meats in addition to the meatballs were added into the Gravy. Beef, pork or sausage were the norm. It could be a combination of them or sometimes all three. It was a work of art.

I still look forward to my wife cooking the traditional Sunday dinner, however, we do not have macaroni every Sunday as we did back then. Today we worry about our weight, high blood pressure, high cholesterol and other health issues, things we were not concerned with in our younger days. But when we do have the traditional meal we enjoy it as we did back then.

The memories of our mothers cooking Sunday dinner will last with us forever.

*Frankie's a master. But next to my mother, come on!*

## Sunday Gravy: What a Concept
### By Dom Capossela

Sunday Gravy in the North End was our Pledge of Allegiance. Making a Gravy showed your loyalty to the neighborhood. Only then you earned the right to call yourself a North Ender.

Of course, everyone's mother was the best cook in the world. But I've got news for you and them: they weren't. It was MY mother who was the best cook in the world. In the many months every year when my family was really destitute, my mother could nonetheless create a Gravy so extraordinary that the taste of it would resonate in our mouths for days, until the next Gravy.

Sunday Gravy began on Friday for us, with a walk out to the butcher to see what credit he would allow her. Maybe a pork butt or sausages, a piece of chuck, and always ground meat. We often had chicken feet (which we all loved and fought over) and sometimes had pigs' feet which we also prized. From time to time, she would get skirt steak to pound thinly, season prodigiously, roll up, and tie: a Braciola. Boy! Did we fight to get our fair share of that.

But whatever the selection of other meat, there were always meatballs. Like the niçoise olives in a Salade Nicoise, the rascasse in a Bouillabaisse, and the turkey at Thanksgiving, meatballs were *de rigueur*, or should I say, *d'obbligo*?

Not that our recipes were precise. Far from it. You might think the meatballs were always all beef. They weren't. We used any combination of beef, pork, veal, or sausage meat. Lots of people added pine nuts. Most people fried their meatballs then put them in the Gravy. Lots of times I talked my mother out of frying them and just adding them into the Gravy uncooked. I liked the textural softness.

Meatballs were the crème de la crème of the Gravy pot and gastronomic sneak thieves, and they numbered in the hundreds, targeted them, sneaking into the kitchen, forking a meatball, and running out to eat it surreptitiously, or brazenly eating it over the pot, while complaining, "It's hot. It's hot." Meatballs were to food snatchers what the Ford F-Series pickup trucks or the Honda Accords were to car thieves. Some might say there was actually a bit of crossover between the meatball snatchers and auto robbers.

After the question of meats was resolved, the other major question was: what pasta shall we cook? Birthdays and holidays meant one or the other of our three favorite pastas: lasagna, ravioli, or gnocchi, all made the hard way, with elbow grease.

*The Royalty of Italian pasta. When the ricotta cheese is seasoned just so, just as my mother seasoned it, and the pasta is the rolled-out, silken home-made version, with a perfect Gravy on top? Lions and tigers and bears, Oh, my!*

My mother's homemade pasta was incomparable. I remember ma taking over our beds so she could spread the homemade pasta to dry. We lived in small apartments. Space was at a premium. On less exalted days, we ate dried pasta. Our Italian grocery stores had many choices. I always favored the large types, like cannoni or tufoli, giant rigatoni.

Sundays weren't universally happy days. Certainly not at our house. We were a contentious family, nasty, full of insults and belittling remarks, unsympathetic listeners. Our meals were invariably delicious, but the Waltons didn't live here.

It wasn't until I was eighteen-year-old and had a waiter's job at the Harvard Club that I understood what a healthy family could be. I was watching a family of five seated, talking, eating, laughing, the children, ages five, seven, and nine. My family had never been to a restaurant and this one, so close up to me, caught my attention. At one point, after they had shared a laugh, the little girl, the five-year-old, fork in her hand on its way down to spear a morsel, said chuckling, "We're a funny family." I slipped away, found an isolated spot, and I cried.

But our food tasted better than others, then and now. When my mother slid the pasta into the boiling water, we were all gathering round with the final touches to the table, the excitement building.

At the appropriate moment the pasta had to be tasted for doneness. This was a mini-event and I, the only boy, was the taster by birthright. I took the role seriously. I forked a piece of pasta from the rolling water and put it on a plate. Then I spooned a bit of gravy on it, sprinkled some cheese and freshly ground pepper. Only then did I taste it. All eyes were on me. I was the Punxsutawney Phil of all pasta dinners. Would it be another minute, or could we sit and eat now? "It's done," I would pronounce. A sigh of relief and we sat and began the feast.

From Friday morning when he went off to work, until Sunday, we saw very little of my father. He'd be out all-day drinking and eating bar food, coming home only late at night to sleep. Sunday mid-day, when the whole North End was home eating their Gravies, my father, alone in the barroom, knew his binge was over and he had to head home and sober up for work the next day. God bless him, he never missed a day's work.

The tasting done, the plates filled, the cheese sprinkled, and the first bites taken, came the sounds and the vibrations we dreaded.

"Boom. Boom. Boom." The sound of my father's very heavy wooden leg landing on one of the wooden steps three flights below. When he was closer we could hear him groaning out loud, "Olga," my mother's name. "I'm sick. Olga." "Boom. Boom."

We continue to eat but the joy is gone. He comes inside the apartment, staggers to the crowded table, sits heavily, and pushes the closest plates and glasses out of his way. What follows now are twenty minutes of his groaning and swearing. Heads down, we silently and quickly finish eating and, singly, get up, rinse our plates, and move out of the small kitchen, leaving Camie alone with Olga who accepted it as her duty to tend him.

Sunday Gravy: a great concept.

*Come hell or high water, every Friday and Saturday a fixed army of street vendors occupied several streets on the edge of the North End, notably Blackstone and Haymarket Square. These stalwarts, braving sometimes brutal conditions, provided the city with fresh produce at below reasonable prices. Many North Enders worked there and earned enough to create a comfortable living for their families.*

# I Do Believe in Magic
## *Glimpses of North End Life*

We've gathered eleven of Sammy Viscione's philosophic and comical vignettes in random order, beginning with an affectionate look back at street vendors of long ago.

## Ten Cents, Three for a Dollar

Shopping malls, supermarkets, internet shopping, box stores; what a transition from Arthur's, Shuman's, La Fauci's, Moscardini's, and Resnick's Hardware, etc.

I never realized the large number of merchants and street vendors there were in addition to the services available to a population of up to 38,000 people living in the North End in the 40s & 50s. What a tremendous concentration of commerce in an area less than a square mile. There was so much for sale, so much buying and so many to service in so little an area. The pushcarts and horse drawn produce carts hawking goods street by street made me wonder how long had man been peddling that way.

What a memorable time. There was the milkman, ice man, rag man, diaper man, oilman, crab man, pizza man ("gowada gowada"), the insurance man and the other man collecting the daily investments.

I remember the weekends, especially the holidays and the abundance of food on display along with the rich aromas and hordes of people streaming down the streets with their plastic coated or 5 cent brown paper shopping bags. Yes, those Italian

*These portraits of hard-working, honest, uncomplaining merchants, here, a man selling chestnuts, fill me with awe. God bless America.*

people doing what no other ethnic group could equal, buying goods and food and later preparing them with the best ingredient, love.

Much has changed now. Once a predominant Italian community is very much diversified today. The North End was the people. Some remain to witness the lost culture and solidarity that once existed there. It will always be the oldest neighborhood in the country but no longer the greatest. Nothing lasts forever. However, one thing our generation learned was that food and appearance were foremost then and remains with us today. Years of experience proved to us that nothing beat wearing a Castignetti Brothers suit while eating a dish of macaroni. Viva the "Nordend" as we would say!

# Anko's Fourth of July

Thank God for summer. Now that the 1954 school year was over and everything academic was left behind, that meant I was able to purge from my mind all that Okie dokie bullshit I had to learn and conform to for the past ten months. Pardon me, but I was an undesirable student. The few months ahead laid promise to good times. And one prominent event that would render such enjoyment was the Fourth of July. I knew the meaning of the holiday and I loved America, but the patriotic aspect of the day wasn't foremost in my mind. I thanked Ben Franklin and George Washington as I did with Peter Rabbit and Santa Claus when I was young. But having no school, receiving free Hoodsies from the city, watching from the Slye Park the US Navy honor America with a 21 gun salute and shooting off our own arsenal of fireworks, then watching the Boston Common firework display from our rooftops was what truly made the day.

Of course weather conditions were an issue. Any precipitation meant disaster. That morning I tuned my radio to station WHDH to hear from Logan Airport the National Weather Service forecast weather conditions from Eastport to Block Island including Narragansett Bay. Once clement weather was predicted we were ready for takeoff. We took inventory of our fireworks cache. We counted the lady fingers, the one and two inches, cherry bombs and roman candles. Once tallied, we were off to Angelo's grocery store to buy Diamond rand wooden matches @ 10 cents a box. We whacked up the expense between us. We then foraged for cardboard boxes, tin cans, etc., for anything we could explode into heaven or blast to smithereens. Our launch site was the Gas House, a.k.a. the Gassy. That expanse of concrete and granite was ideally suitable for Christmas bonfires and demolition work.

It wasn't long after we started to blow everything up God created when we were interrupted by the arrival of Anko and his mangy, mean German Shepherd who I swear was half dog and half wolf. Everyone knew Anko. His name, his looks, his demeanor and family ties made him an outstanding character. He demanded that we all relocate to the third level playground with him. Once there, he revealed a grenade. I thought only the Army and John Wayne had hand grenades. Anyway, he suddenly pulls the pin and lobs it into the lower left field corner of the playground. Bah-Boom! Smoke and concrete dust billowed as we cheered with delight. What a treat! What a guy, our hero. Butchy Costa asked him for the pin, but was refused. Later I figured out why. It was evidence of that criminal event.

The pleasure of that memory suddenly collapsed one day years later while I was serving in the Army. After Boot Camp I was assigned to infantry school where weapon-training is in depth and extensive. Once course covered grenades, the various types and their uses. With each introduction I absorbed the information casually until the type Anko detonated became the subject, then I paid particular attention. I was stunned to hear that it was a fragmentation grenade having a ten second time delay fuse with an effective killing radius of 30 feet releasing up to 3,000 pieces of shrapnel, each with a velocity of 27,000 feet per second which is ten times faster than any bullet, meaning that a fragment the size of a pin head could enter/exit the human body with ease. How lethal I realized only then, what a devastating weapon that foolhardy tosspot exploded near us kids. Although we were probably 25 feet above ground-zero, nevertheless he exposed us kids to such extreme danger.

A year or two later I saw Anko and wanted to recall the incident with him but from a near distance he appeared to be inebriated. Evidently, through his life he was good at drinking but not thinking.

Let me close with the following factoid.

Between the years 1950-54 despite its diminutive size, the North End gave the world its biggest robbery since the beginning of mankind, Brinks, and produced a world champion boxer, Tony DeMarco, and a public Fourth of July human grenade launcher, Anco, (no last name given.)

# The Missing Mickies

Michelangelo Jr. High

Class of 1958

The purpose of these stories is to share with each other those wonderful experiences and happy times spent growing up in the North End.

We all have many, you know them; holidays, dancing, dating, hanging out, sports and those that are private and unprintable. Because most anecdotes will be covered by the aforementioned, I selected an experience of mine that was bizarre, maybe supernatural. I will explain, you decide. So come along and enter the twilight zone as I take you to the Fall of 1957.

At the time, I was attending the Michelangelo Junior High. Because we were Catholics in a public school, we were required to attend Christian learning classes at St. Leonard's Church. Every Tuesday promptly at 1PM, Father Edmund and his aide Stanley would arrive, congregate the 40 or so guys, and escort them to the Parish Hall. That is when the phenomenon started. As we proceeded down Charter St. onto Salem St., taking lefts and rights on different streets, at each turn, the guys started disappearing. First, Murray, Louie Sforza and Toto were gone. Johnny Brad, Gumpsy, Scarpiccio, Guy G. and Buddy Miceli vanished. As we turn into Tileston St., Guso, Frankie Marino, Alie Federico and Richie Gambale were no where to be found. The ranks dwindled as we neared the parish. Suddenly, Carlo De Luca who was to my side seemed to vaporize. I then became alarmed. I tried to find Chippa Venuti, Joe "Delie" Deliberti and Richie Fan, but failed.

Finally arriving at church, no more than 3 or 4 survived. Fr. Edmund was unmoved. He was composed. His aide, standing to his right was transfixed, mute. They both were oblivious to the voids left by the trip. Were they under a spell, demonized?

What happened? Why was I spared? Did my Guardian Angel, which I earned for spending 9 years at St. Anthony's save me? After dismissal the bizarre events continued. Miraculously, the guys suddenly reappeared. First, at Carlo's poolroom, then Minnie's, Mazza's was next, Roger's, Peglegs, Fiore's followed. I couldn't believe it! Thank you, Lord, they're safe.

Fortunately, we lost no one that year. Our class, 9 C-208 celebrated the outcome with a prayer we composed. Let me share. Let us pray.

Dear Lord

Now I lay me down to sleep

I pray to you my soul to keep

If I should die before I wake Bet a dime on 208


# A Lesson In Science

If I had an inclination of becoming a scientist or physicist, I gave that notion up one day while attending Mr. Shea's class at the Michelangelo Junior High School, affectionately known as the Mickies.

Mr. Shea was our Science and Math teacher. To us guys he was commando Shea. That moniker rooted from his military service where he served as a meteorologist attaining the rank of Major. I purposely mention his military occupation because another school related chapter could be written about it. Mr. Shea was a strange sort, a cantankerous person, frustrated and incompetent as a teacher with contempt for us, "God damn little pups." Despite his shortcomings we liked him and respected his service to our country.

Back to Science

One day, in fact as it turned out, it was the only day we had Science as a school subject. Mr. Shea's agenda that day was to explain and demonstrate the principles of combustion utilizing gas emitting from a Bunsen Burner. Apparently, Richie Gambale knew of this demonstration and warned us that Shea had the shakes from drinking too much and watching him ignite the gas while quivering was a scary sight. I remember Bozo saying "fuck him I'm not going to class because he'll kill us all." Richie, our savior, said not to worry because he had a plan. He said that when Shea was about to ignite the gas he will shout out for us to duck. So, when Shea was babbling, we all were waiting for the moment, looking at each other ready to explode with laughter. Suddenly, Shea turns the gas on and as he reaches for the matches, Richie shouts ''DUCK." In concert we all hit the deck! While Shea was cussing and screaming at us, we were pissing ourselves with laughter.

When he bombed out of the classroom, I realized with him he took my only interest of  to MIT. Oh well, I said, maybe I'll become a butcher.

## Puff, Puff That Cigarette

I was 12 years old when I took my first drag of a cigarette. It was early June of 1955. School had just ended. Cody Giovanditto and I bought 2 loose from Charley the Jew's variety store at the corner of Wiggin and Tileston Sts. For 5 cents. Other stores like Pegleg's, Roger's, Piccolomini's and Joe Black's also sold cigarettes to kids at affordable prices. Remember how they used to sell two or three cigarettes for a nickel or a dime? However, each store would give only the second-rate brands like Dunhill, Wings, Sarno, Viceroy, L&M, Herbert Tayrenton, Kent and Raleigh. The latter being a more popular sell since the owners would keep the coupons. Our choice was Kent because of the micronite filter and its reputation for being very mild. The micronite filter was a new breakthrough in cigarette technology rendering low tar and a smooth taste. Just right for novices. By the way, they were popular with women but too mild for real men. So, on one Sunday afternoon, on

*Handsome, muscular young men
surreptitiously growing into premature
manhood. They thought.*

the Bathhouse steps, we were going to do it. Learn to smoke.
Become one of the guys, leap into manhood. But who would
go first? Let's choose up! Finally, we decided to do it together.
We agreed there will be no phony exhaling. The smoke had
to come from the lungs. We each took a deep drag and immediately started to choke our brains out. I coughed so violently
my nose started to bleed while Cody nearly vomited. We went
home sick, embarrassed and defeated. But we were determined.
Finally, after a few more days and nickels we perfected the vice
and entered into manhood.

To His memory:

Robert "Cody" Giovanditto

1944-1972

# I'm A Girl Watcher

Not me but Johnny Damiano. He and his brother, Anthony were affectionately known as the "twins."

Johnny was playing center field for our team, the Remenham A. C. That season we beat out the Christy Club for first place. The Christy's were the favorites to win. Players like Carlo De Luca, Richie Fan, Guso, Victor Passacantilli, Paul Corolla and Benny "Cycki" Farentino comprised a very good team.

The Barnoners won the other division despite being underdogs. However, the so-so talents of Billy Venezia, Lyo, Leo the Lion, Gunga Din, Georgie Macaroni to name a few, prevailed. The Remenhams were a balanced team in both offense and defense. Johnny Repucci, Franny "The Jet" Viscione, Charlie Coppola, Bobby Chiota, Roger Mustone, Cody Giovanditto, Emo Bevilacqua, and our pitcher Davy Fasano, Junior "Flash" Gaudin and myself made it happen. The championship game was close in scoring. The lead changed hands several times to my dismay. I thought we would shellac them for sure. Well, going into the last inning we were leading by one run when they loaded the bases with one out. Gunga Din came to bat. Davey wound up and pitched: Gunga swung and lofted a routine fly ball to centerfield. Then disaster struck. Johnny didn't catch it because Johnny didn't see it. How could he when he was watching the bathing beauties in the pool. Needless to say, we lost the game. I often think of that game and truly believe events like that could only happen in the North End. Johnny remained a life long friend but I never forgave him for the loss.

# Sister, Sister School

"Blessed are those who take us closer to God."

This beatitude absolves me for me the harsh ways and means used by the Franciscan Nuns at St, Anthony's Parochial School.

All were of Irish descent with the exception of Sister Mary Yolanda. (Buon Giorno Sorella Yolanda"). They taught a student body of predominately Italian chidren. They were strict disciplinarians, devoted to their religion, who expected unconditional compliance to authority and God.

I know very well the worst because through the grades I was always sorted into their classes. St. Anthony's had an unofficial placement system wherein the studious and well-behaved were placed into the "A" Class while the reverse into the "B" Class. As noted, I was a perennial "B" because I carried the stigma of being a troublemaker. In fact, my mother once told me that if she had to see Sister Superior one more time she might as well join the convent.

My seventh grade was the hardest because I had the toughest nun, Sister Mary Eileen. She was young, handsome, with cold steel eyes and hands faster that Willie Pep's. She would hand out punishments like they were samples. The most memorable and disappointing event for me happened that year. It was early December when she told us that donated Xmas decorations will enliven the spirit of Christmas while dressing the classroom…wonderful! That afternoon, during break, Delie, Cody, Alabama, myself and Pucky D'Ambrosio went to Faneuil Hall Market and 'appropriated' a Christmas tree. With excitement, pride and expecting lots of kudos, instead, Sister told us we were not allowed to help trim the tree since we did enough already to taint it. I learned instantly that crime does not pay and that she was a Spartan. Not even the birth of Christ would soften her. Everyday until Christmas that tree stood there to remind me of my stupidity. I couldn't bear witness to it.

*They were not watching "All in the Family."*

It was a long way to June. The book reports, extra homework, the detention periods took their toll, but I survived. Many people maligned them. I never did. I got what I deserved. I respected these women married to God, sworn to poverty while living a cloistered life with no social existence. Sadly, a few years after leaving St. Anthon's, I was told that the handsome, young Sister was called to heaven.

# North End Martyrs

Turn backward, turn backward,

O' Time in thy flight

And make me a child

Just for tonight.


Will that be sufficient time to make amends and thank Ms. Dennison, Herrick and Pagliuca. Remember them? The Librarians on North Bennett Street.

There, these dedicated women avail themselves to everyone seeking guidance through the myriad of books shelved on two floors.

In our teen's, the Library was merely a social center, a pool room with books, a place to hang around after school or after supper on cold winter days.

A place where wise guys had laughs at the expense of the librarians, driving them crazy.

I'm sure their salaries were far from munificent and we certainly didn't help to compensate it.

Ejections were common.

Miss Dennison, in her everyday blue dress showing us the door, while Ms. Herrick was leveling suspensions as we exited.

One day, myself, Charlie Coppola and Victor Passacantilli were recalling to mind our past teachers and civic leaders.

The Library came up.

Suddenly, Victor started lamenting over the things we did to nettle and abuse them, in particular these women.

Victor's words grated on my mind.

I began to feel equal to his ruing and embarrassment.

Fame or shame could be inspirational and that's what encouraged me to remember them and hope for all those they helped during their many years of service to our community, they will always be a credit to them and their memory.

Thank you ladies.


# We Want Lenny


The thunderous chant was first shouted in the early years of the Friends of the North End Reunion. The halls of the VFW, the North End Union and the neighborhood health clinic on North Margin St. would tremble until Lenny Gambale went on stage and vocalized his renditions of "That Old Black Magic" and "Up the Lazy River." His voice and gestures emulating those of Frank Sinatra and Bobby Darin brought down the house. The guys loved it. Encores were no longer requested but demanded. Lenny was composed because he had experience. Through his teens into his twenties that was Lenny's thing, singing. Street corners, pool rooms, gymnasiums and dances were his stages, in fact, anywhere, anytime Lenny would give you a few lines. In those years he was handsome, svelte with blond hair and impeccable in appearance. Throughout the day he would constantly monitor himself. Mirrors, glass door reflections and compliments were his best friends. He was a narcissist with an ego and desire to make it big time. However, his association with Ronnie "Lefty" Fuccillo and Mario "Scanlon" Siciliano affected his career causing his demise. The year 1972 was the first reunion for the Friends of the North End. It was a nonevent for Lenny. The first few times Lenny delivered smoothly. Subsequent years not so well. Finally, the guys were disappointed and started to boo him. The next year he failed again to please the crowd and was pelted with bread and boos. Later, along with boos and bread came the coffee creamers and dinnerware. At first, Lenny stood center stage until finally succumbing to the barrage and dashed for cover behind the honorees. Gigs at the reunion ended drastically when Anthony Tomasone threatened him at gun point. Publicly his career had a similar ending after a performance at a Revere Beach nightclub when the owner informed him that if he ever returned there he would be shot.

He was an unfortunate kid who dreamed of Las Vegas but ended up in Pal ookaville. It's all behind him now, but I know he still looks back. He and I sometimes fairytale about how things could have been for him if only for a little luck. Lenny's singing career didn't last but his enduring years being a great guy, friend and gentleman have. As far as I am concerned and others will agree, Lenny will always be our star. Nice try, Lenny. We love you.


# Tamarindo

I get to thinking often about the years that have passed, of times when I was young, and the memories I now cherish. I framed them by activities, family, friends and unusual events. One recollection that stands out is the living conditions which we were subjected to. The population residing in such a housing density,  exceeded physical boundaries. However, rents were affordable. With virtually no recourse and little opportunity to draw succor

We struggled along therein.

Economics, searching for value for the cost of items purchased was an absolute focus . Seeking affordable pleasures was a relentless pursuit. One however, that I enjoyed along with many others was a 10 cent glass of tamarindo soda sold at Burdens pharmacy located on Hanover st. The subject beverage was

*Cool and refreshing, yes. But anomalous to the era. Tamarindo was not well-known in either Italy or America in the 1950s. How did it get to the North End? I'd tell you if I knew.*

concocted from blending tamarind syrup with soda water.

So it happened one summer day when I, and five friends, with baseball gloves on hand embarked on foot to Fenway park. After playing catch in Fens Stadium, and prior to the Red Sox game, we went to the near by Hemenway drug store for a refreshing beverage. Because we all favored tamarindos , we ordered six. The prissy looking gentleman who was to serve us was totally unfamiliar with our request, and asked us where were we from, and what is a tamarindo? He then very politely told us that beverage was probably indigenous to our Italian ethnic community. We all thought a tamarindo was common like 7-up, coke, root beer etc , and available throughout the the USA.

I learned somewhat then And more so subsequently,  how naïve and parochial our upbringing was living in the north end.

Well, a few years later while being employed by a electrical contractor my assignment one day was to install contemporary lighting at the Hemenway drug store. The excitement I realized of possibly reuniting with that gentleman who introduced me/ us to America would be a forever moment. Sadly, his absence was disappointing. I failed to thank him for teaching me that

75

beyond Hanover st. Existed another life.

Oh well, life went on.

## Do You Remember?

Do you remember that North Station paraded circus and rodeo shows on Causeway Street?

And that one minor aspect of living in the Copp's Hill area was incessant interrupted sleep due to the neighborhood cacophony . If it wasn't the overhead screeching of the elevator trains it was fog horns blaring. Or boat whistles, and freight trains clanging . If you worked nites and slept daytime, as i did  it was because of the  jackhammers or mother's yelling.

Growing up I remember  the smell of sol naphtha ( suffa nappa) and pine sol emitting from the recently washed stairs and side-walks.

-Police patrolling while checking store locks
-The Blue Goose police paddy wagon.
-Free hoodsies compliments from the city on the 4th of July.
-Visiting 4 churches during Holy Week.
-Women hanging out washing windows..
-Day travel camp.
-Swimming with the Jelly fish along the barges and pier.
-Best dressed on Easter morning
-Burning Xmas trees in the Gassie.
-Eating hot chicken soup on hot summer Monday nights.
-Having to be home when the lamppost came on .
-Picking up horse chestnuts in the cemetery.
-The horse stable.
-Library puppet shows,

-Brinks robbery.
-And the champ Tony DeMarco.

Sadly, time passes on and much is gone, but precious memories linger and live in our hearts.

# Personalities
## *Adding to the Magic*

People make a neighborhood; characters season it.
And we had our fair share of those...

## A Cornmeal Heirloom
### By Lisa Pasto Gurney

What I always noticed first when Josie cooked were her hands. Her fingers were slender but gnarled, and from the base of her knuckles to her wrists they were swollen with arthritis. I often wondered how she could create such amazing dishes with these two distorted tools.

Josie was my surrogate grandmother. Related to my family through marriage, she had been in my life since birth. Being Italian and living in the North End, food was as big a part of our lives as loving and breathing. Josie taught me everything she knew about cooking and wanted me to develop a fine repertoire of dishes as much as she hoped I'd grow into a good and decent woman.

I had just turned twenty when she announced it was time for me to learn how to make cornmeal pizza. I didn't know how to react. I had been asking her to teach me for years and she always refused, claiming I wasn't ready. And now the moment had come. Why? I wondered. What changed? I didn't ask her though, afraid to jeopardize the moment. Instead, I jumped up to get the cornmeal.

"Heat some water up in a small pan," she said, ambling to her plastic-covered kitchen table.

While we waited for that to boil, Josie shook a generous amount of cornmeal into a bowl, added a fistful of grated Romano cheese, and a few shakes of black pepper.

"How much of each are you using, Jo?" I asked.

"You don't make this with exact measurements, Mumma. Just watch," she said as she mixed the dry ingredients with her hands.

She always called me 'Mumma' when speaking with me directly, and 'the baby' when speaking about me to others. I would remain the baby well into my thirties when she passed away.

Next, Josie uncorked a glass bottle filled with green-gold olive oil and drizzled it over the dry ingredients. The pungent scent of oil blending with cheese made my mouth water. She scooped up a portion of the semi-wet mixture and pressed it into my palm, our hands joining in a mushy prayer.

"Can you feel how this is starting to stick together but it's crumbly too?"

I nodded. She smiled and moved to retrieve the hot water.

Adding the water was tricky. I knew this because I had heard her curse once after using too much. She poured it into the middle of the mixture, forming a gritty well, then handed me a spoon.

"You mix first with a spoon because the water will burn your hands," she instructed. When the water was absorbed into the cornmeal, she said "Now, start mixing and pressing with your fingers."

She watched intently as I rolled the wet cornmeal around, pinching here and there.

"This is the most important part, the consistency," she said. "It's where everyone I've tried to teach has gone wrong. It has to be wet enough to hold together, but it can't be too watery, or it will fall apart when you fry it."

My throat dried as I furrowed my brow. The mixture was warm and heavy when I closed my hand around it. When I released my grip, it seemed to settle and relax at the bottom of the bowl, but not fall apart.

"It feels good, Jo. Moist but...strong."

I struggled for an accurate description as her hazel eyes bore into me. "It feels wet enough to hold together, but pasty and firm too."

She lowered her own frail fingers into the bowl. I waited, holding my breath.

"Brava, Mumma," she said with a solemn nod of her head. I exhaled. The hard part was done.

We fried the cornmeal in olive oil, bringing it to a golden tan on either side, and then cooled it on a glass plate lined with paper towels. In Italy, the pizza would be served under greens; spinach or Savoy cabbage with beans sautéed in garlic and oil. But I always loved to eat it plain, and still do, so the subtle cornmeal flavor amid the sharpness of the cheese is not lost.

Less than a week later, I made the pizza without telling Josie. I wanted to surprise her, and if I failed, she never had to know. I agonized over each part of it; was there enough cheese? What will happen when it comes time for the hot water? Finally, becoming exasperated, I just relaxed and let touch guide me. When the pizza was done, I wrapped it carefully in plastic wrap and then in tin foil like Josie did. I gently placed it in a brown paper bag.

I tried to calm the rush of my heart as I walked the three blocks to her house. When she answered my knock, I had to hold back from shouting. Instead, I said softly, "Jo, I made cornmeal pizza."

Her eyes glimmered with surprise. "

You did? Let me taste!" She broke off a piece and bit into it.

I couldn't hear a sound as she chewed; the world seemed to

*Nothing says lovin' like cutlets in the oven...*

stand still. "Mumma, this is delicious...buonissima!"

My heart leaps whenever I remember the look of pleasure and admiration she gave me.

Josie's picture is pasted to the side of my refrigerator where I see it every time I cook. Whenever I make cornmeal pizza, I reach over to kiss her and thank her. I can't say my pizza always comes out perfectly, but when it does, I billow with pride, and I know she is somewhere watching, proud of me too.

Josie's Cornmeal Pizza

2 1/2 cups of cornmeal

3/4 cup of grated Romano cheese

1 teaspoon black pepper

1/2 cup olive oil

3/4 cup hot water

Mix cornmeal, cheese, and black pepper together. Add olive oil and mix. Slowly add hot water, mixing first with a spoon and then with your hands. Form small patties (about 2 1/2 inches in diameter) and fry them in olive oil in medium heat (about 2-3 minutes on each side) until golden brown.

# Joe La Fauci
## By Joe Sarno

Few are left who remember Joe but those that are still around who knew him will never forget him. He was a giant of a man both physically and intellectually. He was a willing and most capable teacher of math, Latin, Greek, history, religion, opera and current events and everything else, it seemed. He had a considerable personal library.

His father was a fruit peddler and sold watermelons on a horse and wagon on our beloved streets. I can still hear his father's shouts of "Watermelo, Watermelo." Joe Jr. as a teenager assisted him and sat at the rear of the wagon. One hot summer afternoon he fell off the rear of the wagon and as he lay on the ground he was taunted by some neighborhood kids because of his size. After that incident he became a recluse for the most part because of that. I cannot remember him further away from his doorstep than Tony the Butcher's at 156 Endicott, Maria Libra's Salumeria at 159 Endicott, DeLeo's Drug Store at 151 Endicott owned and operated by a wonderful woman named Mrs. Morriss or Rossi's Florist shop just a few doors down in the opposite direction.

In the late 50s I entered a contest with the Boston Herald or maybe it was the Record American. Each day they posted a photo of a celebrity and a clue and you had to identify each of them. The early photos were very easy to recognize and of course as the contest approached the 96th and final photo, they became difficult, partially obscured and to me impossible. I would run to Joe and he would say, "It's Otani, he's a Japanese shipbuilder" or "This is Ernst Lubitsch, a film director." I won $75. More than a week's pay for many families at the time. I offered Joe half. He refused to take any of it.

On a typical summer afternoon Joe would be sitting on his doorstep listening to the radio. One of his favorite programs

*Wonderful people contribute to the*
*magic*

was "Stump the Staff." People would submit historical, geo-
graphical, political or current event questions to the radio staff
of 5 experts. If you stumped the staff, the station would send
you a 5-pound Colonial ham in the can. One afternoon after
completing an errand for him, I went up to his apartment to
bring him whatever he had me buy and was astonished to see
that he about 30 of these hams. He gave me one and I ran home
to give it to my mother. She was delighted. The only question
he posed to them that I can remember was who preceded Haile
Selassie as ruler of Ethiopia. Joe used many pseudonyms and
eventually the radio station barred him.

Joe earned some of his living by creating crossword puzzles.
Some were published in the New York Times.

When St. Mary's school announced its closing in the early 70s,
like many others, I fled to the suburbs for the sake of my children's education. I had been busy raising my family and hadn't
seen Joe for several years. I ran into Joe coming down Endicott
near Cooper far from usual range. He had lost a lot of weight
and looked great. We chatted quite some time. We parted. I
smiled. Joe had gotten his life back.

# Lama, Our Brother
## By Joe Sarno

On behalf of the friends of the deceased, we offer our sincerest condolences to his son Robert, his granddaughter Janessa, his sister Juliette and her husband Robert, his brothers John and Anthony and his wife Jeannette, his in-laws, his nieces and nephews and grandnieces and nephews and his cousins. To us his friends, he is also our brother perhaps not in blood, but certainly in closeness and affection and yes love. Our loss runs very deep as well.

Leonard Tammaro. Some of you say "who?" Yes that's Lama's real name. I, by accident of fate was present at his 2nd Christening. I can't remember the date but I remember that it was good weather. I remember the place right in front of Tony's butcher shop, the Boston Meat Market. Maybe Lenny was 10 or 11 possibly 12. The late Joe LaFauci, an enormous man in every aspect, particularly enormous in intellect was there standing with us. Mr. Lafauci had a range of perhaps 100 feet from his front door which was further down Endicott St. in the building where MangiaMangia is now. The butcher shop was just narrowly within his range.

Lenny and I liked to listen to him. He often held court in DeLeo's drug store at the corner of Endicott and Thatcher in the same building that the Tammaro family resided.

Mr. LaFauci and Fr. Bouvier, a Jesuit at St. Mary's, often had discussions or debates. Once, Fr. Bouvier, I recall took the position of the Catholic Church and Mr. LaFauci took the position of Voltaire on some important topic of Catholic dogma. After some time they decided to switch positions and continued the debate for another half hour or so. Lenny and I looked at each other in admiration and amazement. We didn't have a clue as to what they were talking about.

*Often disrespected by the priests of the
Order, Brother Gerard was constantly
on the neighborhood streets begging
money for this or that charitable
cause. A saint, he.*

Not to be outdone, Lenny would show off his intellectual
prowess outside the drug store by studying the racing form, a 4
page fold-out that listed every race at every track in the country
with the horses names and the jockeys and their post positions
for that particular day.  Lenny would study it for a few minutes
and give it to me or whoever else might be there.  We would
ask "the 3rd race at Pimlico, what was the horse's name?", "the
jockey?", "the post position?" And he would answer correctly
of course, every time.  Then perhaps we'd ask "the 8th at Hia-
leah?" and he would answer it right again.

There were maybe 500 races for the day.  After a 3rd correct
response and because we were all so competitive, someone
would say "OK who was the trainer of each of those horses?"
Lenny said very calmly "Oh, you want me to do trainers too?"
Give me back the sheet for a few more minutes.  Totally frustrated and because we knew he could do it, we said "ah let's go
play errors."

85

Back to the Christening, Mr. LaFauci on that eventful day put on his serious face and studied Lenny. You have dark skin and very soft facial features and after a very long pause said "My god you could be taken for a young Dalai Lama." It immediately stuck. We didn't know what on earth was a Dalai Lama.

Over the years a few people would ask me, how come he was nicknamed after a South American llama. I would say "please there's only one L in his nickname" and leave it at that.

In those early years, we played in Thatcher Court, Douglas Court, Lynn St., North Washington St and Medford St. There was Bobby, Brothey, Cibo, Frankie, the other Frankie, Fudgie, Junior, Phil, Richie and Ricky. We went to St. Mary's. We were altar boys. We played tag, wrigleys, errors, stick ball, buck-buck, releavio, 123 red light, tops, kick the can. We collected baseball cards and pitched them on the sidewalk against a wall.

We had fruit fights, and snowball fights with the kids from Stillman St. We told stories to scare each other. We raced in the streets. I was sometimes Swaps and he was Nashua. Other days we reversed the names of the horses. We went to the Lankie, the Scollay and the Bowdoin. We reenacted every fencing movie and every war movie. Lama was our brother. Nobody can change that.

As we got older, we hung out on Endicott St. We added to our entourage Anthony, Benny, Bobby, Bochie, 2 or 3 Butchies, Cochie, Davey, Dennis, 3 or 4 Joes, Joel, Joey, 2 Johnnies, another Frankie, Freddie, Lenny, a couple of Louies, Matty, Michael, Paul, Richie, Ronnie, Salvy, Sammy, Spin, Spitzie, Tommy. There were others. Please forgive me if I missed someone.

We went to bachelor parties, baseball games, basketball games, hockey games, prize fights, amateur fights, wrestling matches, barbeques, picnics, weddings and movies uptown. We went to Hayes & Bickford for coffee. We went to Burden's for Tamarindos. We went to Polcari's on Salem St. for lemonade. We went to Dippy's for sandwiches. We went to the Regina for pizza. We went to Tecce's for dinner. We did so many,

many things together.

Then there were the older guys who taught us so much and how to behave and how not to behave. There was Abigail, Biffo, Big Bobo, Little Bobo, Bozo, Brazzie, Cabbage, Cheege-lo, Chip, Danno, Hippo, Eddie, Eddie Boy, Joe, Joey, a couple of Johns, Jimmie, Lefty, Leo, Lubo, Miele, Oboy, Pat, Paulie, Shy, Sonny, Tony, Vito. They were our uncles. They looked out for us. We were their nephews.

Some of us got married and moved to the suburbs. Lama was still our brother. Nobody can ever change that.

Lama then moved to Florida and we saw each other less. The separation meant nothing. We saw each other less frequently. But so what. We loved our brother and he loved us.

Lama was not only smart, he was fun to be with, happy, gen-erous, kind and always showed interest in his friends' lives and families. When we were very young, he was smaller than most of the other kids and was often the object of practical jokes. He always took it good-naturedly and smiling. He was a joy to hang around with. Yes, he had his faults. We all have them. But he taught us a lot. Endicott street guys were sharp, streetwise and very smug. But, you know what, he was smarter. In reality, we benefited from him. We all became smarter and wiser.

So many years have passed through our fingers. So much has happened and now that we're in the December of our lives, we can all look back and say "we all loved him then and we love him now."

Several years ago, I was in Como, Italy. I was casually walk-ing around the city one morning when as I walked by a mag-nificent church in the center of town, I saw people leaving the church. It was a funeral. None of the people were crying or mourning. They were smiling and chatting. When the casket was brought out by the pallbearers, the people began to clap. They weren't feeling sorry. They were congratulating him for his life.

I clap for you Lama. You lived your life your way.

We miss you brother. Godspeed.

## Ron Fuccillo's Story
### as Told to Dom Capossela

Ron Fuccillo is the quintessential product of the North End of the era. Not only did he grow up with us, he went to the same schools as we did, grammar school at St. Anthony's Catholic and high school at Christopher Columbus. His best friends, and he has a lot of us, he has known for seventy years.

His teen-age years he hung out on the corner. Not a group of tough 'corner' guys, just boys playing all kinds of ball: errors, stickball, half-ball, and on and on. Playing sports so factored into our lives that Ron swears we didn't learn to dance or hang out with girls until it was almost too late. In retrospect, despite the reputation the North End had as being dangerous to visitors, we had very little contact with the police. We kept our own law, our own order, and our streets were the safest places for women and children.

All those years in close proximity to the same group of kids, about fifty of us, led to the adoption of the same set of values. We did things together, many of which we've written in this book. Some good deeds. Some rascally. Some just plain stupid, like when Ron led a small group of high school sophomores to run away from home. On the spur of the moment. When they finally arrived at Logan Airport with no money and no food, they spent five minutes agreeing it was time to return home.

Ron was a hard worker and, after high school, took on a series of jobs, often two at a time. Hard work and ambition and determination. Ended up as a surveyor until, in 1965, at age twenty-two, he was drafted. He served a tour in Vietnam in Camh Ran Bay, on the east coast of that country.

*Learning the ropes from big brother, Ben*

He enjoyed the opportunity to give back. He believed that community service, defending one's country, and loyalty were part of his makeup. What America is all about. A true North Ender.

Other than a bout with malaria, he came out of the army unscathed. He returned to school and got a degree in computer science.

On graduation he went to work for the state and stayed there all of his life. He met his wife,

(recently deceased), bought a house in Everett, and raised four children. The family has expanded to include six grandchildren, three boys and three girls. To supplement his state salary, Ron took on second jobs, including a valet. Like the rest of us, Ron wanted to be a good father and a good husband. Hard work didn't deter him.

He loved being a father, another shared North End trait. He attended as many of his children's games and school events as he possible could. And he learned how to cook. Of all of his accomplishments, he's most proud of his family.

Here's a quote from Ron:

"I would be remiss if I didn't mention holidays and ALL informal events, were shared with the entire family at grandma's house. This is where I learned to love. And respect all our family traditions. and customs. Which I'm So proud to be part of. I hope I've made my family proud, as I lived by these rules and also passed them on to my children, who in turn passed on to their children."

God bless you, Ron.


## Josie, A North End Housewife
### By Victor Passacantilli

My mother, Josephine Grasso was born on August17, 1917 in Riesi, a small paesi in the Province of Caltanissetta, Sicily. She came to the North End in 1920 with her parents and 2 sisters.

She left the Michelangelo Junior High School after the 9th grade to go to work in the clothing industry to help support the family. She worked in a sweat shop sewing padding by hand into the shoulder sleeves of women's dresses.

She married my father, Albert in 1938 and from 1941 to 1957 she gave birth to six sons. Most of the rest of her life was spent caring for her family as a wife, mother, and housewife. She was the heart of our family, always "there" for us as my father continued to work hard albeit downstairs in the Blue Front Restaurant.

On Saturdays, she would assign her sons chores before they could leave to "go out and play." We scrubbed the stairs, swept the floors, made our beds, dusted and polished the furniture.

Our evening meals were feasts and Sunday afternoon dinners are still an indelible memory.

As kids, my brothers and I caused more than enough mischief and confusion for her. Yet, she was steadfast and could mete out punishment with the best of disciplinarians.

*Mother keeping family intact*

It was not until my father passed away in 1988 that she would emerge beyond her role of housekeeper and mother to show her 6 sons another side of herself. She then started to display traits that had gone unnoticed. Her intelligence, "street smarts" and her intuition were forthcoming. At first, I was surprised by this unveiling but came to realize what an amazingly wise and beautiful woman she had always been. She had been encapsulated in a man's world for her entire life and never given an opportunity to show her whole self beyond the role of a housewife and teenaged wage earner helping to support her family. The women of her generation in the North End remained in the shadows, providing unconditional love for their families, standing at the stove cooking, washing and hanging out clothes to dry, and hidden behind a pile of laundry to be folded and ironed. Very few were given the opportunity to reinvent themselves, yet most North End housewives seemed content to remain in the shadows.

May God bless them all!

Shall I compare thee to a summer's day?

Thou art more lovely and more temperate.

Rough winds do shake the darling buds of May,

And Summer's lease hath all too short a date.

Sometimes too hot the eye of heaven shines,

And often is his gold complexion dimmed;

And every fair from fair same time declines,

By chance, or nature's changing course, untrammeled:

But they eternal summer shall not fade,

Nor lose possession of that air thou ow'st

Nor shall death brag thou wand'rest in his shade

When in eternal lines to Time thou grow'st.

So long as men can breath, or eyes see,

So Long lives, this and gives life to thee.

Sonnet 18

By William Shakespeare

# The Dream of Socrates
## By Ralph Indrisano

My relationship with Socrates started when I was twenty two, and continues to this day. At that time I was a hopeless drunk and street punk who was going to quickly graduate to a drug addict and criminal. It was a time of deep debauchery in my life. No only I did not care at the time. It was much worse than that I did not care. I did not evencare that I did not care. As a matter of fact I really liked the lifestyle of being a drunk and a burgeoning drug addict. I was twenty two and I could see no future for me so what did I give a fuck. Getting high was wonderful and I loved the boys (the Goombas) from our Streets in the North End.

The North End was like a giant Fellini movie and you never wanted to go home because we were afraid that we would miss something. Nobody was like anybody else maybe everybody was a nobody in the North End at that time and they could be anybody they wanted? Not only was everyone a character but every character was different. You had a cast of characters that was tantamount to a Shakespeare play. I remember Fat Ronny and myself as well as twelve other denizens of the North End. We were about to go drinking in the back of the Stillman, an Alley which was perfect for getting smashed nobody lived there so we can yell and sing all we wanted. I was carrying a fifth of Jameson Scotch Whiskey in a brown paper bag stupidly not holding the bag at the bottom. The Brown Bag broke with its content on the sidewalk on the corner of Copper and Endicott in front of Joe's Candy Store. There was silence as that precious liquid flowed not in our mouths but on the sidewalks of Cooper Street. Then, Fat Ronny said, " Quick grab the straws.". It would of been a time of mourning and anger and maybe even a fight instead because of the eloquence of Mister Fat Ronny to being a memorial moment that was full of laughter. I still remember it now decades after it happened with fondness and warmth.

It was the height of the Vietnam War and as far as I was concerned I was going to Vietnam to die. And, I had a lot of evidence to back it up. Out of the myriad of beefs or streets fights in the North End and Boston Trade High School, the worst high school in the city of Boston. I hardly ever won a fight in Boston Trade or the North End and there was plethora of them. I figured if I kept up my record in the mean streets of Losing fights and getting my head busted. I took some pretty vicious beaten-s, two in which my mom did not recognize me when I walked through the door. It was Tutto Finito. (Italian for all finished). By some miracle I got into the National Guard and my tour of duty in Vietnam and death was postponed . I was going to a different kind of horror.

The Army and especially Basic Training was a strange place. It was actually a lot like the North End. They both were teaching you to be tough, and to kill people if you had to. There were differences. You had to conform to a different hierarchy in each structure for indoctrination. In the Army it was blind obedience to authority: in the North End it was blind disobedience to authority. Any revolt to authority was smashed in the US Army. In the Mean Streets of that Italian enclave, We celebrated revolts to authority. In the Army, Cooking was not like your Momma's back home in the North End. In the Army as a matter of fact it was a diametrically opposite.

Another similarity between the US Army and the North End was that You learned to be part of a tribe that was separate from the social structure of the society. I remember My Friend Marvin Levin saying to me who fought in the Battle of the Bulge when I asked him was it patriotism that got you through that hell. He said no. Marvin said that what gave him the courage to endure survive and serve with honor was what him and the rest of his comrades feared the Most which was that they would fail our comrades. Marvin said he would rather die than do something that would result in the death of one of his fellow soldiers. It was true of most The Boys from the North End as well. In some ways we became soldiers of a different kind.

On my first weekend of National Guard Duty after coming

back from Basic Training to do the rest of my military obligation, I had to do my first training weekend for the National Guard. I was in a two and a half ton army truck going to our training Camp on Cape Code with two fellow national Guard soldiers who were also MIT professors. We were the only ones in that truck. They were talking about some pretty heavy shit. We were only allowed to go twenty five miles per hour and it would take us five hours to get to our base camp in Cape Code from Commonwealth Avenue Boston.I thought I was getting a college education in the back of a two and a half ton army truck. You gotta remember who I was in the back of that truck with those two MIT professors.

In the sixth grade after I had Polio. This was in the mid fifties when polio was spreading like a pestilence across the United States. It was as my therapist who would say decades after that having polio was a a knuckle event an event that moves your life in a completely different direction. I remember taking good care of my appearance before catching and recovering from Polio to not washing and not brushing my teeth to wearing school uniforms that were to say the least sub standard. I went from an honor student in Saint Mary's Elementary School to a silent extremely withdrawn failing academically student. I stuttered. I do not know if it was from Polio I had it in the throat or from the anxiety of the trauma of having polio. I was mis diagnosed as being retarded by the good sisters of Notre Dame . The High School because I stuttered. I went to Boston Trade School which was the dumping ground for students with learning and or discipline problems in the Boston Public Schools System. We started out with 48 students in the cabinet making class and seven graduated and two of the seven who graduated could not read.

But in spite of being denied an education the conversation we had in the back of the truck fascinated me no matter how erudite it was. I just listened for five hours without speaking a word. I often wondered was there a destiny that was ruling my ends, some accident of faith, that changed the course of my life.

It was Saturday night after we set up for camp, and one of the professors was really drunk. I was not drinking, I do not know why. I never before missed an opportunity to get smashed. Maybe it was the conversation on the truck that stimulated me enough. I remember going to the head to take a wicked piss when one of the professors who was in the truck with me, in the middle of the night. he seemed to be walking out of darkness as he came over to talk to me. To my surprise, he was very direct and this was not an abstract conversation. He told me that he envied me. I said why you have a beautiful wife a great family, great job and a world class education. When you compared our lives his seemed so highly advantaged to mine. I was not even having sex during a sexual revolution and a street fighting man from the NE who was destined to get shot or prison or drug addiction. He on the other hand had this American Dream life upper middle class secure and privileged life. Wife house kids the full catastrophe.

What he said next really touched me. He said that he envied me because I had a huge capacity to love and he did not. I Knew he was right about me having a great capacity to love. I do not know how the fuck he knew it because before he spoke to me I did not know him at all I did not know that I had a huge ability to love. He told me that on the surface I was happy but deep down I was depressed. He said that all I wanted to do was intellectual and creative things. He said I should take drugs and the drugs would act like a catalyst for me to see my depression and then act positively to something creative and healthy. Then, I would realize that all I wanted to do was do intellectual and creative things. I listened and went to my tent. My first thought after he said that was, What the fuck,I might as well as start taking drugs which seemed to appeal to me most and see what he was saying made any sense.I ended up getting out of the National Guard for medical reasons just after a few months after this conversation .

After about six months after getting out of the Guard, I thought that I would try out what this mysterious professor from MIT said. Being a reprobate, they idea of taking heavy drugs appealed to me so I did Drugs first. In the North End they were really sub species of North Enders in the genus family of North Ender-s . You had a sub species that managed to do well in school and go to college and manage to not get addicted to alcohol drugs or criminality. Then, there was a sub species that was addicted to alcohol and did not do well in school. Then, there was a sub species that were addicted to Heroin. We kinda gravitated to each other. There were some crews or tribes that were co-mingled they were drug addicts and alcoholics and non- alcoholics. There were few people that did not drink it all. There was some crews that had no drug addicts at all. There was one crew or tribe that was composed of all drug addicts.

Drinking and drugs was a sort of religious passage for us. Instead of water to be baptized we used alcohol and blood we fought a lot for our Baptism. (Meaning an act, experience , or ordeal by which one is purified sanctified, initiated or named) of quite a different kind . Then, I started to take Acid every week as my first choose of hard drugs. I found it interesting that we were always in the same crew. Actually, I am in the same crew now. I do not think if you asked anyone from the North End who grew up when I did would say that they are in the same crew. If anything was going to separate us it would of been half of the boys on the corner going hip taking drugs dropping out and those who went straight. I never experienced that those who were straight did not care for me and we were not a part of the same crew that meant in the North End a certain kind of band of brothers. I do remember being judged and I remember a concern I never experienced any hostility from my crew. There were other crews that were intensely hostile. There were actually people who were shot and beaten because they were going hip. The thing was I think that it was too cool to be hip at that time and that ameliorated a lot of hostility.

After about three months from June to September after taking the acid I realized that he was right about the depression because I fell into a deep depression which I was avoiding for most of my adult life with drugs and alcohol. So I decided, what the fuck I might as well read some books maybe he was right about the intellectual and creative aspect of what he was saying. There was a problem about doing that. In my house we rarely read and there was only three or four books available. Three Philosophy books. One was the Dialogues of Plato and the two others Marcus Aurelius the Mediation's and lastly Saint Augustine Confessions. My younger brother Joey sent away for them about a million years ago and there they sat on the book shelf attracting dust.I choose the dialogues of Plato. I knew that this was the Book that I had to read. The book pulled me towards it like a magnet. What was it that pulled me toward the Dialogues of Plato and Socrates?

In the North End it seemed to me that education was something that you got to pull yourself out of poverty. I remember Doctor Mike when he saw me reading a book I was taking a course in called Problems in Philosophy that the problem of the Problems of Philosophy was Philosophy. I do not know if he was saying that because he felt that learning philosophy would make a person too conceptual or that getting an education in anything but to make money was a mistake.

I remember being told constantly when people asked why you going to college I would say that I loved it and the response was invariably something to the sense of get the fuck out of here or why are you doing something like that, or what is wrong with you, Why the fuck you taking courses. You gotta understand at this time this was the second book that I would read in my twenty two years. I only read one book in Trade School. And that was because when we went to class one English Teacher had us read it in the class. We never did homework: I do not remember anyone taking a book home from school. The Book in that English class was Twenty Thousand leagues under the Sea.

When I was in grammar school because I stuttered and had ADHD and at that time they thought I was retarded so they just passed me from year to year. I read all that evening and around eleven pm I was finished. I was amazed by two things one that I completed a book in one night and the Rotherham that there actually was a person when people were going to put him to death unjustly he said in his reply , " I honor and love you but I would rather obey God than you." At that time if you stepped on my toe I wanted to kill you and almost killed a couple of people because of something just as trivial. I was just amazed by this. How can a man say this, and I felt I knew that what he said was in full earnest to those who sentenced him unjustly to death to say as his first response I honor and love you? I went to Catholic School and they taught us of a man called Jesus who taught unconditional love and forgiveness for every one. He too forgave those who put him to death and loved them who crucified him. I always felt that they the Priests and Nuns were trying to shove this down my throat. It never meant anything to me. It was just a myth for me. On the other hand Socrates was flesh and blood and I felt I knew him personally when I read The Dialogues of Plato I felt that I was with Socrates holding his hand as he went through his what he had to go through. I felt a kinship towards Socrates. In some unconscious way he was a surrogate father taking the place of my Father who died just two years ago. I think that maybe he was hitting upon something in my collective unconsciousness in some way.

The second thing that Socrates said in the Dialogues of Plato that really throw me around the world in twenty days, was that a man could have anything he wanted health, wealth and happiness if he merely told the truth. Now, at the time I lied cheated, stole, and did anything to get what I wanted. Only for my family, friends and the tribe that The North End was that I belonged too and only felt a belonging to where the only people that I had any sense of integrity and morality. Socrates was saying that we should love all people and be good to all people that morality and integrity was vitally important in a person's life. This was the exact opposite that I was acculturated to which was compromising your morality in situations where you were dealing outsiders, people outside of the North End to get what I wanted was okay.

As I finish the Dialogues I was intensely galvanized. I just could not stand still. So, I went out for a walk. For the first time, I did not walk in the North End but around the periphery. The time passed. I walked in what we in the North End called Ghost Town the deserted area by the Waterfront. Then, to my surprise I started to walk out of the North End down the financial district. The streets of the financial district at that time before the gentrification of Boston were deserted and so was Ghost Town. The only people I saw were homeless drunks. Down through the Combat Zone I walked. Then, I started to walk through the Public Gardens something I never did just living a half hour walk from them. This was like a whole world opening up to me. As I walked down these green streets lined with trees down Commonwealth Ave, there was grass and trees and tall granite buildings and no tenement fire escapes where only one family lived.

Unlike the North End where multiple families of ten and eights lived in small apartments with no grass and trees. It was funny I was not jealous or even bitter that people could live in so much affluence and we did not. We had an affluence of a different kind. I remember talking to Jerry Ameno, Captain Carl's father. He said that the NE was a special place. I asked him why. He said that the love here was just amazing. Jerry was an architect who somehow managed to achieve this in the Great Depression in a depressed area he was also stigmatized because he was Italian. I was down the North End Pool with JR and Mikey Fud and we were talking about how crazy the North End was and this young boy who could not be over eight said, " Hey, I know the North End is crazy, but I would rather live around a bunch of people who are crazy and love you than people that are. not crazy and don't love you. Out of the Mouth of babes.

I did not know how far I walked: when I started to head home. I just remember being at Government Center under an abstract statue of Thermopylae commemorating that battle between the 300 Spartans and the mighty army of the Persians, For those of you that do not know of this battle the Spartans fought till the death and the King of the Spartans said before they were killed ,King Leonidas, " Go tell to Sparta, thou who passest by, that here, obedient to her laws, we lie." And so I sat under Thermopylae. It looked like a brass dinosaur that was also a greek warrior a Spartan symbol for the battle of Thermopylae standing on three legs. I remember, I remember that there was no thoughts going through my head. There was only a certain

kind of silence and calmness that seemed to flow from inside
me which I never experienced in my life as I looked towards
the east were the sun was beginning to rise. I have never stood
up all night to greet the dawn without sleeping even when I
was taking acid I would sleep for two or three hours.

Then, suddenly coming from outside me a thought that seemed
to come not from me but was me said to me. I am going to do
an experiment. We, will see if this man called Socrates was
bull shitting us or was being straight. I will start to live my life
telling the truth and loving and forgiving all those around me
unconditionally. I knew that I wanted this more than anything. I
embraced the commitment and promise that I was going to live
as well as I could and die as well as I could like this Man from
Athen's who somehow in some way I did not understand was a
father to me. Not knowing what the fuck I was doing. I figure
that if knowledge was virtue and virtue was essential to leading
a good life I should go to school.

And so I began my Odyssey Towards Socrates. I worked hard
and went to school nights. I had to take a train ride to Roxbury
the African American part of Boston in the middle of the race
riots to get the basics so I can go to college. Then, I went to
therapy Know Thyself at twenty five and went to college after
two years of picking up what I did not learn in High school.

Then, at twenty six nothing was seeming to work. It seemed
like I was banging my head against the wall. I was working
marginal carpenter jobs that were really miserable jobs. I was
going from one armpit of construction to another. I remember
one night I parked my car in front of the Pizza Regina. Out
of all the parking spaces I parked in I remember parking that
night in that space in mid November still. When I woke up
the next day to go to work, I found that my car was broken
into and the tools stolen. I was devastated I fell into an abyss
of hopelessness and despair. Before I went to bed I thought of
death. Thinking maybe I will get lucky and not get up to do this
tomorrow, tomorrow, tomorrow again and again and again.

Sleep came hard, but I did succeed in succumbing to deaths

counterfeit I bore deep into unconsciousness. There I had a dream. It was the beginning of a golden dawn and I was walking down a wheat field in full bloom a golden wheat field of hope all around me. As I walked down this path in this sea of Golden Godlike Sunlight and wheat I could see a figure of a man walking toward me. As he came closer I recognized and knew that he was Socrates. He was wearing a himation which was a simple two piece garment around the body. I was stunned and did not know what to say and much to my astonishment he said in a Heavy North End accent. "Hey, Kid how you doing." I felt completely at ease in this strange twilight One experience. I felt like I was talking to one of my brothers from the North End. I said I do not know Socrates I am trying so hard to do as well as I can and live an honest and noble life like you lived and it seems so hopeless. It seems that for me that the streets are just too long. I will never forget when I looked up from the ground when I could pick my head up from looking at the ground and saw his smiling face. He said in perfect NorthEnd English. " Don't worry about a Ding Kid. You are going down Da right Path." And then, he pointed down a earthen path surrounded by golden wheat and the sun was beginning to rise at the end of the path. I felt that all was well and all well be well.

I was in a state of euphoria for about six months. How I viewed the world shifted from a mean spirited place where I could not cultivate a life to that Life that had the possibility of being rich and fertile and more importantly I experienced being fertile. Because I of this I was more responsive and optimistic to my life and life in general.Now, as I enter my seventh decade. I find that I am still committed and work on Being Socrates. I am a lifetime student. I go to therapy and do transformational courses to know myself. I have been going to an ongoing poetry class for over twenty five years which I have been doing in the Boston Center of Adult Education. I still read and work on my ethical and spiritual self. Socrates is a constant presence "an ambassador from another world a world of pretty marigolds of two shades which he announces not knowing what he does other than walk the streets of Athens holding the flowers upright as a torch so early in the Morning."

I remember the second and last dream of Socrates when I was going through a tough depression over thirty years ago. He said to me as he said to those Athenians as he saids to all human being for all time . A man who is good for anything ought to calculate that death is not an evil this truth - that no evil can happen to a good man ,whether in life or after death. And the God will not forsake the good man either in life or in death. I remember being uplifted much the same way I was uplifted with my first dream of Socrates. There are no regrets not one.

Now, I am seventy the same age of Socrates when he died and can see death approaching and still long deeply to say and mean as he said and be as he was so so long ago. I find that this is all I ever wanted only this one thing. I hope That I can say before I lie in my grave. Stranger go tell that Athenian of so Long ago you who passed by that here I lie obedient to the promise to Be Socrates so long ago."And I have promises to keep and miles to go before I sleep and miles to go before I sleep."

I Promise.

*Everybody had their own story. Given the powerfully charged atmosphere of the magical neighborhood, some of the stories are more poignant than others.*

# Observations
*Going back in time.*

Several authors share their insights and knowledge to take us
back to that warm and vibrant place.

## Remembering
### By Gus Pesaturo

The Nuns

For those of us who attended parochial school and in the North
End there were three, Saint Mary's, Saint Johns', and Saint Anthony's. The closest to Hull Street was Saint Anthony which I
attended. Franciscan Nuns ran the school and taught subjects
like history, geography, and mathematics. I would say they did
a pretty good job considering 10% of my class could not speak
English, only Italian.

I had lots of problems in school, for one I hated school! Second, I had an appendix attack and had to miss one full year.
Having a year off and coming back was very difficult for me.
My best subject was recess. The nuns sold cookies or should I
say windmill cookies. The small milks we got from the school.
The class sponsored children from other countries which
were collected weekly, and it was putting change in the Mite
Box. My seat was changed because the nuns wanted to keep
me close to the front of the class not because of my grades
but because I was easier to hit and closer to the closet which
I spent lots of time, sometimes hours. It was not all that bad;
I ate cookies and drank lots of milk! The nuns decided that

the closet was not a good idea so me and Nick LaRosa were selected to push a cart to the marked shops to pick up the fruits or meats. Nick carried the list, and I pushed the cart. Nick also spoke good Italian which helped but the majority were Jews which if I remember gave us the most of what was on the nuns shopping list. No money was given, it was donations. Amazing every week this mission would happen. I was always under the impression that the nuns would receive a bill, but Nick told me the true story. The nuns sent us with a list begging for items. The nuns were tough, my hands would be red from the three-foot ruler. I used to get hit, I deserved it. Today the nuns would be put in jail for brutality. Today when I see a nun, I always say hello and God Bless You.


The Sandwich

I attended Charlestown High School in the late 1950's. It was like attending a school that did not like "North enders" let alone Italians. Most of the time spent in school was for subjects and the second half of the day was shop. I wanted to learn a trade, Electrician was my trade of choice, and it was a trade that paid good as well as the opportunity for side jobs. My mother would always make me lunch to take to school. My favorite was Italian tuna and either potato or asparagus with eggs, they were fried the night before but ready for my lunch the next day. Tuna fish sandwich was with mayo and always on Italian bread. My mother considered white bread a killer for the body and teeth. One day we would sit in the gym or out by the Bunker Hill Monument with my new friend or should I say acquaintance. He was working as a long shoremen in the hole of a container ship. O'Brien or OB as he was called. We would have lunch together. OB was well known with the other people living or working in Charlestown. This day we ate at the base of the monument. I opened the wax paper off my asparagus and egg sandwich. Remember it was fried the night before. The brown bag was oily. I did not care about the bag, I wanted to bite into that sandwich. I noticed OB was looking at my sandwich, he said "what the are you eating grass?" I said, "what do you mean OB and what are you eating in hard white bread?" I told him you should not make fun of something you have never tried. After he stopped laughing, I offered him half and he offered me half of his. I asked what he was offering, and he said it was corned beef. I had never heard of corned beef. OB said, "are you kidding?" Me, I said no I was not kidding, and it was between two slices of white bread that was bough yesterday from a day-old factory for ten cents a loaf! So sure enough I ate it and OB ate the asparagus and egg. From that day on my mother made two asparagus sandwiches, one for me and one for OB. I was not ready to eat white bread. I did not want to die or be killed by my mother.

The Good Old Days

Last week while working towards Shaws Supermarket next to The Garden the day after the Celtics lost in game 7 to the Miami Heat 103 – 84, a sad day…. I noticed a group of kids playing basketball. For those of you North Enders its where our beach used to be. Lots of good memories. Well let me tell you my good North End story all of us born in the 1940's will remember.

I was born in 1941 in The North End. My Family building on

*Polluted? We had great fun until they closed it. The pool that replaced it was pretty fun, too.*

7 Hull Street. By the way the front door was never locked. In 1949 – 1950 I had an appendix attack, in fact it burst inside of me. I was driven to Childrens Hospital emergency room which was the start of a four week stay to clean out the poison in my stomach and digestive system. Now back to the north end beach. Exercise was my prescription leaving the hospital. My mother walked me from Hull Street to the beach every day. I walked and walked. If it was a very warm day my mother watched me swim. Today the water would be called polluted. Why? Because of the oil spilled from the Navy ships coming into port for repairs. I would push away the oil slick with my hands and making sure my mouth stayed closed for fear you would drink oil. After swimming for maybe fifteen to thirty minutes I would get out of this water and walk home with my mother to take a bath. That is what I remembered while watching these kids playing a game of 21. The piers are gone, its all in the past or as they say, "the good old days." The North End is not the same, I walk the streets everyday between three and four miles six days per week not seeing anyone I know, yes it has changed.

## Remembering
By Diane Pesaturo

Once upon a time we all had 4 rooms, maybe 3 people to a bed-room, a toilet in house or hallway and local bath house. Most parents had their own room. Ours was the kitchen with chipped porcelain stove and refrigerator.
Once upon that time we had one mile square with the Gassy, Prado, and Copps Hills Cemetery We had nuns, priests, and public schools.

Who Knew     When my grandmother passed away that the cozy (Chicken coop with windows) four room apartment that I shared with my father, mother, and brother would expand to include my grandfather and spinster aunt.

*Three to a room? We made it work.*

Who Knew    My little cot would now become a sofa bed to sleep my aunt at the head and me at her feet at four years old. My brother would relinquish his room to my grandfather and inherit my cot.

Who Knew    That this living arrangement would pass well into our young adulthood.

Who knew    That this was not the norm because almost every North End family lived like this or close facsimile.

BUT

Who Knew    How amazing a life this was! Friends, families, sharing apartments for meals and holidays. The greatest foods ever cooked. Curbstones for playing errors, cars to hide behind for scatter, building for support for buck buck, sewer covers for marbles, Tops, and skating in the spring, converted to scooters in the fall. Sneaking into the social clubs to watch the older teens dance at the canteen night and longing to be old enough to be there.

Who Knew    It wasn't normal that every Saturday my father, grandfather and brother had to leave the house so my aunt could open her rubber bathtub while my mother (the saint)

*While washing stairs was mandatory, neighborhood clean up was volunteer only. But everyone joined in. If you didn't, you might be the victim of a maledizione, a curse.*

*Worse than a simple maledizione, someone might hold down her middle and ring fingers with her thumb while extending her little and index fingers, pointing this mano cornuta at the shirker, calling down misfortune on her. While the Sign of the Horns is universally used in Italy to ward off evil, locally we sometimes used it to curse someone.*

would boil water on every gas jet to fulfill her baby sisters one pleasure, a hot soaking, instead of the usual sponge bath at the kitchen sink. Factory work was not a clean job!

Who Knew    Or who will ever experience the sound of scrub brushes on the wooden steps being washed away by every tenant on their apartment level or the strong scent of sophana-thol coming down the hallways onto the sidewalks and into the street by the landlords doing their part to keep their property clean.

*A term of renting was that every week*
*every tenant washed her stairs with a*
*disinfectant.*

Finally Who Knew    That the joy of watching my mother stretch her starched lace curtains on racks fastened with little nails, notice the sparkle on freshly washed windows and waiting on the hallway steps while the wax on the kitchen floor dries and the ultimate closure of the evening running into the living slash bedroom to lie on my fathers stomach listening to gurgle while he enjoys Sparky, the Gillette razor parrot on the Friday night fights.

*We had marble collections that we coveted. We added to or subtracted from our collections by playing on sewer covers. Note that the streets were so safe, so well-guarded by every resident, that three-year-old children were sent 'downstairs' to play without a specific adult with them. Reminds one of the Japanese series about two and three year olds called "Old Enough." Of course, mothers were constantly looking out their windows to ensure their safety.*

Who Knew great….! This is how it was Once Upon a time and it was

## Memories

I woke up early, looks like another great day.

I can feel the heat of the sun on my face when I go out to play.

Friends on every corner looking for something new to do.

But it looks as though we're destined for games we're used to.

Marbles on sewer covers protecting cables below ground.

Roller skates opened to attach to a board. Fastened to the crate making a scooter to ride on.

Found my Yoyo and Top hadn't used them in a year.

But couldn't find my baseball cards. Oh yes, I lost them playing, I fear.

Time is fleeing now the sun is going down, as I hear a familiar tune, acapella groups are beginning to croon.

A few more steps now and I'm home at last.

Another great day, what a movie it would make, and what a great cast.

## The Good Life
### By Frankie Imbergamo

I am writing to share my experiences growing up in the greatest neighborhood in the world. the north end of Boston MA.

I grew up on the lower end of hanover st. the block from Giros restaurant to charter st. this neighborhood section was amazing.

everyone watched out for each other--like we were all family. my fondest memories was playing all sports playing in the north end park--little league--my brother and I played for bova bakery--it was so much fun and then we played at the bath house gym on our basketball team the north end stars!! we were very good in sports--not bragging but our basketball team came in first and second place many times.

growing up in the north end --on saturdays i would go with my mother and grandmother food shopping around the north end

*It was a group effort but led to a very long late night event with people dropping in and out to snack on a favorite.*

and at haymarket. that was a great experience cause then we went back to our house and made the gravy-Sauce to probably most people but we always called it gravy--when u put meat in to a red sauce it became the sunday Gravy!! plain sauce is marinara. I learned how to cook from my mother and my grandmother rose.

they were both excellent cooks. we always used the freshest ingredients. I treasure those days--cause what I learned how to cook enhanced me to write a cookbook the Good life favorite italian recipes. In 2005 I entered a national cooking contest on Emeril live--the foodnetwork enetering my recipe from my cookbook frankies gravy and meatballs. there were 1500 contestants and I was chosen the top winner and appearing on emeril live where emeril lagasse recreates my recipe plus 3 other winners. that was a life changing experience. Getting back to my roots there was nothing better than to wake up on a sunday morning with the aroma of fried meatballs--my brother and sisters would all try a meatball before we go to church. most of my fondest memories was right downstairs from out apartment as we got older we hung out in the blue front restaurant which was owned by my friends the Passacantilli family--great people. I remember on saturdays people would come in with an empty pan and they would fill the pan with homemade tripe for like 3 dollars--unbelievable you will never see that anymore!! my north end has changed now with only like 10 percent italians but we lived in the greatest part of the country and best neighborhood the north end!! there will never be a neighborhood like the one I grew up in. the good old north end.

in the block I grew up in there were many merchants where today there is only very few. from commercial and hanover on the corner was Giros Restaurant, net door was Marios deli, then the hbl social club. sullys sub shop.

then Joe solimine bakery, blue front, the coin A matic is still there. then the Boston I grocery store,then demasi meat market, charlie buicks tobacco store and on the corner of charter was Dicks Vegetables. across the sreet oon lowere hanover was the shell gas station, serrechias coffee shope. shortys barber shop. Pals Bakery. dotties bus stop coffee shop corner of battery, anastasi photo shop studio, Pandolfs tailoring, bella napole restaurant beninati grocery store phils candy store, joe king travel agency and then gurente funeral parlor. the good old north end!!

## My Memories
### By Anthony Tony Antidormi

I often think back to the days when I was growing up in the North End and the fun we had swimming at the North End Beach before the pool was constructed and watching the older boys diving off the pier. This double deck pier is where we would spend hot summer nights to cool off. Not far away was

*When you can't afford a bike you take a crate from Haymarket, steal a skate, and, with a hammer and nails, it's better than a bike.*

*That goofy boy with all the girls is me.*

the Coast Guard Base where they would show us kids free movies on the ship's deck. I lived off Commercial Street where the freight trains would travel through late at night disturbing many a good night's sleep.

Our days would be consumed with making scooters out of pear

*But just as I say,*
*It takes judgement, brains, and maturity to score*
*In a balkline game,*
*I say that any boob kin take*
*And shove a ball in a pocket.*
*And they call that sloth.*
*The first big step on the road*
*To the depths of deg-ra-Day--*
*I say*
*Friends, lemme tell you what I mean.*
*Ya got one, two, three, four, five, six pockets in a table.*
*Pockets that mark the diff'rence*
*Between a gentlemen and a bum,*
*With a capital "B,"*
*And that rhymes with "P" and that stands for pool!*

boxes, roller skates, and 2x4s. We would play games like 'buck buck," "relivio," "stick ball," or "errors" or making tents out of cardboard boxes we picked up from the warehouses on Atlantic Avenue. Sometimes at night we would go for a Regina pizza and hear Connie, the waitress cursing was a real treat.

Hygiene meant that my mother would put clean underwear in a bag and send me off to the public bath house to shower. She would then go to buy fresh fruits and vegetables at Johnnie D's Market. There, if she ran short of money, he would tell her to pay when she could. That's the kind of trust people shared with one another.

Early a common sight was seeing earnest people with their brown lunch bags going to work and hearing the rag man calling for rags while others, weather permitting would be hanging out their laundry building to building, roof top to roof top. Afternoon activities at the Shaw House in the Industrial School were always enjoyable as was watching Sunday morning gambling going on at the corner of Salem and Sheafe Sts., better known as Cozy Corner.

Living in the North End meant our social centers were the streets. Although our entertainment was creative it was somewhat crude. Our motivations and inspirations came from our love of family, our heritage and devotion to God and our Country.

## Games We Played in the Fifties and Sixties
### By Lino Viola

As a kid, I would play handball, stick ball, punch, and errors with one of two types of balls; one was a pimple ball and the other a star ball. I preferred a pimple ball over a star ball much like a golfer would choose a Titleist over a Nike golf ball. The pimple and star balls were white in color and the same size, but the pimple ball had more elasticity and seemed to travel farther when it was hit, where the star ball was made of a heavier rubbery consistency and not offer the same type of bounce. There was a third type of ball called a pinky, pink in color, which was smooth and a little smaller than the pimple and star ball. Girls played with the pinky ball.

The pimple ball got its name I guess by the raised pimple like indentations that were all over the ball. The difference was the star ball had a star on the north and south pole of the ball in place of the pimple. Both balls also had to my best recollection five thin raised ring-like ridges that went all around the ball. The ridges and the pimples gave you the opportunity to put various spins and effects on the ball, whereas with the pinky, which was smooth, you could not.

*Our recreational lives depended on a steady supply
of these balls. If you had no money to pitch in to
buy one, you felt like a jerk and a freeloader. It
sucked.*

Back in the late fifties we would buy these balls at Joe's Variety store which was at the corner of Cooper and North Margin Streets. The variety stores then were typical mom and pop type stores that one would go to supplement their normal grocery shopping. We were there so much that Joe and Mary, the proprietors of the store, were an extension of our own family. These stores were the precursors of the Store 24s of today but on a much smaller scale.

A Day would not go by where I did not stop at the store at least a few times. This was the place where every kid in the area would stop to get their daily sugar fix. The store was strategically located about twenty yards from St. Mary's Grammar School and had as its main attraction a large assortment of 'penny candy.' The penny candy assortment of twenty to thirty diverse types was in a window display on the Cooper Street side.

You see, the old timers already knew about product placement well before it became the science that it is today in many stores. You could not walk by the store without being enticed by the sweets in the window. There were three to four hundred kids attending St. Mary's Grammar School in its heyday and

I would venture to say that 99% of those kids would stop at Joe's to purchase some candy either to or from school daily. You could also go to Joe's to buy a tonic. A tonic was what we called a soda back then. It was also the place where we bought our balls. I recall that pimple balls cost a nickel then inflation set in and went to a dime and eventually fifteen cents.

We chipped in to buy the balls, and I must confess, given the fact that the statutes of limitation have passed, when we had run out of money would occasionally resort to stealing balls. It was easier to steal off Mary than Joe. You knew when Joe caught someone, because you would see him come running out of the store with broom in hand yelling, "You little bastard!" It was difficult to hold on to a ball for more than an hour before either losing it or breaking.

If a ball was hit or thrown into Mrs. Pino's yard, we would never get it back. She did not appreciate us playing there, so she had a high fence put up around her small yard which she kept locked. We were a nuisance to all the people that lived around the Clinic, especially the ones that lived at the end of Baldwin Place. Mr. Cecca owned the building that took the most abuse from our ball playing. The side of his building that faced the Clinic was windowless except for one skinny rectangular window on the extreme left-hand side on each floor. We used his building to play handball off. We even took the liberty of painting a white line three feet off the ground that went the entire length of the building. This line served a dual purpose; it signified the net for handball and a demarcation for a home run when we played errors. No matter how much yelling and screaming he did at us, he knew that he could not get us to stop playing ball against his building.

One day he took down the wooden framed screens that covered the lone windows and replaced them after he had pounded about thirty protruding nails on the frame of each screen. He knew we could only afford to buy so many balls in a day, so he was hoping that any ball that was batted against one of the screens would be susceptible to getting punctured and rendered useless.

So, between Mrs. Pino and Mr. Cecca we started to lose balls at a faster rate than normal, and you could only steal so many balls before Joe caught you. Even Joe made it harder by moving the placement of the balls to a more secure location in his store. The only kid that was successful at stealing the balls from this new location was Tillie Rags, one of the fastest kids in the Clinic. Tillie Rags' streak finally ended and he got barred from Joe's Variety. Imagine getting barred from a Variety Store.

One day, bored from not being able to play ball, as we were hanging around and fooling around with a couple of dead, punctured pimple balls, I took out my frustration on the ball and ripped it in half at the seam. Now I had in my hand two halves of a ball. As I looked at them, I got mad and threw one of them away in disgust. We noticed how the half of a ball sailed and traveled Frisbee like (this was before Frisbees were in vogue or invented) for about thirty feet. The other kids that were looking on decided to try to duplicate it. Some could, but others could not get the half ball to go more than a few feet. With some practice, most of us got the hang of throwing the half ball. It was different. We could not use it for handball, nor punch, nor errors since there was no bounce to a half of a ball.

Since we had little to do, we decided to try using it for stick ball. Over time we were all playing half ball. The half ball did not travel as far but we learned to have fun with it just the same. It was fun experimenting with the unusual ways you could throw the half ball. You could make it curve in either direction, you could make sink and you could also make it rise starting it from one inch from the ground rising as much as three or four feet all based on how you held it. It was easier striking out your opponent playing half ball. I do not know where half ball originated, but if it were in Boston, we would owe it all to Mr. Cecca and Mrs. Pino.

The Clinic was where I hung out. The Clinic was a building that the city owned and at the time housed dental and medical offices for low-income people. The courtyard behind the building was where we played, and it was also a bypass used by people going from Salem St. to North Margin or Endicott

Streets. It was not a large area, but it served our needs, and it was safe because it kept us from playing in the streets. Whenever we needed a larger area to play in, especially for stick ball, we would venture a couple of blocks over to the Gassy on Prince St.

The Gassy was huge in comparison to the Clinic. You could easily fit at least 40 Clinics in there. Since this was not our home turf, we knew that we could be tossed out at any time by the local kids. The unwritten code was that you did not barge in on someone else's hang out and start playing, you would ask for permission. We were on good terms with the kids from the Gassy, so they accommodated us most of the time. Our biggest hurdle was getting by a tough guy named Anco, who was affiliated with the mob. You could hear Anco's loud raspy voice from a few blocks away as he patrolled the corner of Prince and Snow Hill Streets. You had to go there on the way to the Gassy. He was a lookout for the Angiulo's, who headed the mob at that time. As a kid, you knew how to stay away from him and his dog. You could tell that he was missing a few screws. He loved to scare the kids and you would occasionally see him yelling and chasing after someone with a bat in hand.

This one square mile area, the North End, which was our world, was small but it had approximately twenty different hangouts for kids. Many were schoolyards, i.e., St. Anthony's. the Eliot, Michelangelo and others were playgrounds or just open spaces like the Charter St., Foster St., and North Square playgrounds. The North End Park had two baseball diamonds which were used by all, but only a small percentage were enrolled in organized ball such as little league. I remember the park curtailing the career of many a prospective big leaguer.

The North End Park was unforgiving with an infield that was a mixture of dirt, sand, pebbles, and rocks. I saw many infielders get hit by a batted grounder which took an unsuspecting hop after hitting one of the rocks. No matter how many rocks you would go around picking up and throwing out there always seemed to be another coming out just behind it.

122

For the many that did not play any organized baseball there was always the competition from playing groups of kids from other playgrounds. Kids from the various playgrounds would get together and produce a schedule of games. One night we would go to St. Anthony's to play them, then the next night the kids from the Gassy would play us in the Clinic. Just like the regular baseball games we would have a meeting of the captains of each team to go over the ground rules at each of the playgrounds.

It was quite impressive for a bunch of kids in their early teens to initiate things without parental involvement. We communicated without the use of cell phones. We used our voices and our feet. We were not lazy. You went to your window and yelled at a kid playing below or nearby to give a message to bring to a friend in another part of the North End. You did not use your phone because all the kids were outside. Each of us also seemed to have a keen sense of hearing, especially when our mothers or fathers would call us to come home. There could be five Anthony's playing together, but when Mrs. Ciampa called, you knew which Anthony she was looking for.

The game that I enjoyed playing most was errors. Errors was played with a pimple ball that was thrown against a protrusion of a building. If you had enough kids for two teams, you would play running bases which meant that once you struck the ball against the wall you would run to first. The bases were a combination of manhole or sewer covers, and ones that we painted on the ground. Umpiring our own games created some of the biggest disagreements and fights.

The reason I enjoyed playing errors was because I had very quick reflexes. I was not a tough kid and I never liked to fight, so the only way I got respect was making the tough kids look sick when they played against me. Because I could humiliate them at that game, they never bothered me. I wish that I had the foresight to keep one of those pimple balls for they provided us so much fun and enjoyment at a time in our life when we had so little, but in retrospect, we really had a lot.

# Haymarket
## By Nick Dello Russo

There has been an open air public food market in the Haymarket Square area since Colonial times. In the early 19th century the market vendors were mostly Irish and Jewish but by the 1880's Italians had taken over and throughout the 20th century the Haymarket was virtually all Italian.

The market days were Friday and Saturday. Vendors would set up their stalls early in the morning after loading up their trucks at the Chelsea wholesale market. The market spilled over into the North End and down Salem Street all the way to Prince Street. Italian families from all the streetcar suburbs would return to the North End markets for their weekly shopping.

I was born in a tenement building at the corner of Salem and Cross Streets in 1945, just before the end of WW II. On the street level of my building was a fruit and vegetable shop run by the Tecce brothers. On Friday's and Saturday's they, like all the many other vendors, would take over the sidewalk and street in front of the store and set up displays of their produce.

There were still horse drawn wagons delivering meat and produce in the North End when I was young with a stable on North Margin Street. The stable was guarded by a cranky old man who chased us kids out when we peeked inside to see the horses which were kept up a ramp on the second floor. The wagons were on the street level.

A few doors down Salem Street from my building was a well known shop called Dairy Fresh Candy owned by Joseph Matara known to all as Joe Candy. Joe was originally from the West End and I got to know him pretty well. I once commented to Joe that I thought West End girls were very attractive. He countered saying he always thought North End girls were prettier. Maybe, but Joe married a girl from the West End-as did I.

*Rich with the good things in life.*

For many years Joe was president of the Haymarket Vendors Association and constantly fought with the city and Boston Redevelopment Authority who had ambivalent feelings about the Haymarket. As the area around Blackstone Street became more attractive to developers the BRA wanted to move the market to a less conspicuous location. They suggested moving the market underneath the elevated expressway or down Canal Street near North Station. Joe fought these attempts and, with the help of our North End city councilor, Freddie Langone, and

State representative Sal DiMasi, got resolutions passed to ensure the continued existence of the Haymarket.

Market days were street theatre at its finest. There were organ grinders, one with a Capuchin monkey, entertaining the crowds of shoppers. The monkey had a small round hat which he would hold in his hand to solicit donations. Rumor was the monkey was also trained to pick coins out of pockets but I never had much money so I was safe. At the corner of Salem and Cross Streets was a guy who sold boiled crabs from a pushcart, small ones for a dime and large ones for a quarter. He sometimes had periwinkles which were ten cents for a bag with a pin

*So many sights, smells, and noise, so much crowding and pushing. What fun!*

to dig out the meat. There was the old man who sold slices of pizza and another guy who had quahogs on the half shell. The street vendors would loudly call out advertising their wares just like the open air markets in the streets of Naples.

"Come an get 'em, five for a dollah."

" Hey lady, over here. Nice ripe tomatoes."

"We got the good ones, nice and fresh."

"Looka, looka, looka, I'm giving this stuff away."

The market guys could make a weeks pay in just two days. Tough work, especially in the winter, but the payoff was great and left plenty of time for a second job or a trip to Suffolk Downs or the dog track. My friends who used to help out at the market used to stuff coins inside their socks to add a bit to their pay as long as they didn't get caught.

At around 7:30 on Saturday nights the vendors would begin lowering their prices so they wouldn't get stuck with too many leftovers. You had to buy in bulk, a sack of potatoes or a case of oranges for pennie's on the dollar. Poor people and the owners of low-end restaurants would scour the Haymarket looking for bargains.

When the market ended around 8:30 there would be mounds of trash sometimes ten or fifteen feet high. The city would send trash trucks and front end loaders to remove it before the rats came. Groups of us kids would have the best rotten tomato fights until the cops chased us away.

Across the street from my house on Salem Street was Giuffre's fish market. At the end of the day they would throw out fish guts and heads in wooden crates filled with sawdust. My downstairs friend, Gene-Boy and I would throw fish heads into the passenger side windows of cars on Cross Street leaving the Sumner tunnel. In those days before air conditioning cars would always have their windows open during the warm months. The drivers would yell and swear at us but couldn't stop and hold up traffic. We were fresh North End kids.

Sometimes my friends Charlie Petito, Peter Catizone and I would "borrow" a pushcart from under the expressway where they were stored. We would go around the trash mounds and collect the discarded wooden boxes that were in good shape. We would sell these to the various box companies located on Fulton and Commercial Streets. The small plum boxes were the most valuable and we could get ten cents each for them. Orange and pear crates were only worth a nickel but those we used to make wooden scooters. Every summer we would make a new wooden box scooter with tolls skeet wheels. We would decorate the front with tonic (soda) bottle caps. Old Mr Polcari had lots of bottle caps in his Coke machine in front of his coffee store on Parmenter Street.

One summer I worked for my father's friend, Eddie Simone, in his box company on Commercial,Street. Dom Capossela later had his restaurant in that building. Every morning I would drive around with Gaspar in a box truck. We would go to all the local supermarkets, collect their empty boxes and bring them back to the shop to be repaired and resold. The fish crates were the worst and smelled awful. It was backbreaking work and furthered my resolve to stay in school, get an education and someday have my own business. Working for someone else was a losing proposition.

The Haymarket has changed over the years. Italians still own many of the stalls but now they are joined by Asians, Latinos and Africans. Meat shops that once sold kosher products now sell Halal meat. The vendors are different and the shoppers are more diverse but the Haymarket lives on. I will say that the quality of fish was much better fifty years ago than what I see there today.


## How Could You Tell If He Was Italian?
### By Lino Viola


Step back now to those thrilling days of yesteryear (50's and 60's) and see if you can answer this question: In high school how could you distinguish an Italian boy from the rest?

You may have said:

1. By his swagger

2. Or even by his clothes

3. How about his DA haircut

4. By the olive-skinned complexion

5. Or by the gold chain and crucifix around his neck

Yes, those are all good indicators, but think hard because there was ONE sure fire sign that told you someone was Italian.

OK, if you have not gotten it by now you never will.

Answer –he was the kid carrying the brown lunch bag with the (olive) oil stain on the bottom.

I bring you back to 1961, the basement cafeteria of Boston Latin School; at that time an all boy's school with a strict dress code and discipline; a school that taught you time manage-ment by giving you the least possible amount of minutes to get between classes or suffer the pain of a misdemeanor mark; a

*Better sandwiches could not be found anywhere on earth.*
*Great bread, imaginative ingredients, love, time, and effort*
*all poured into them. One bite and you'll be licking that*
*dripping oil like ice cream.*

school where a good percentage of students were of the Jewish persuasion and Latin was required for all six years, that's if you started in the seventh grade - Oh, the abuse those poor sixies (seventh graders) took from the upper classmen.

Peek into a window of the typical short lunch time a student had (it was about 23 minutes). I would meet a group of kids from Eastie and the North End for lunch and we would sit at a long table. Over to our right were the non-Italians. You could tell them by their neatly folded and creased little flimsy brown bags (bags bought specifically for lunches) made to house two slices of Wonder bread with either one slice of bologna and cheese or peanut butter and jelly. That brown bag could be neatly folded and reused for weeks because the contents did no harm to it.

Like many of the other Italian kids, our brown bags were big, thick and sturdy, for in their previous life they probably carried a few loaves of bread or a few pounds of peppers or onions, you know the number 15 industrial strength bags and weren't so neat looking – no nice crease folded in but a top that was rolled up as best as possible and oh yes, the (olive) oil stain that by 11:30 had really permeated the bottom.

When an Italian kid was about to open his lunch bag the whole table to the right would go quiet, a precursor to the E F Hutton commercial of today as all eyes would turn to see what you had brought for lunch. Well number one you knew you had no Wonder bread but a corner of a bastone or slices of scali or French or even a nice spacchi roll. This was wrapped in waxed paper that was very oily by this time and thankfully your mom had the foreknowledge of what this would look like five hours later and would always include some napkins (oh, God Bless them for they thought of everything). Inside this delicious bread was for most times the previous night's leftovers. One of my favorites was sausage and broccoli rabe and eating one of those required using both hands. None of my sandwiches were ever cut diagonally nor could they be easily handled by two fingers as were those perfect ones that the other kids had.

We had eggs and whatever combination; with peppers, or potatoes or onions etc.; all kinds of omelets between the Italian bread. Veal and eggplant parmigiana, meatball subs, and cold cuts, etc. My mom was afraid that the cold cut sandwich would be too dry by itself so she always put something oily in the middle such as fried peppers for fear that I might choke. Friday was the day that you couldn't eat meat, and if I didn't have a frittata I would have tuna - no, not the one packed in water, but the Italian tuna (Genoa or Pastene) which was packed in, you guessed it, olive oil.

These were the days before plastic wrap or plastic containers so the bread became the conduit for carrying part of last night's meal. Sometimes I would feel bad for some of those very pale white thin kids and give them a piece of my sandwich, a sandwich made enough to last you if you had to stay after school or got delayed on the T. Mom was always thinking ahead.

Our bags could not be recycled like the others and there were some drawbacks to having such a lunch. One was that the afternoon classes were a killer because my full stomach would often cause me to doze off. The other was that you had to be careful carrying your lunch, especially on a packed Green Line train. You did not want to have that sandwich smashed because you

*Mikes Pastry, Boston, Mass*
*Victorgrigas - Own work*

*This shop is iconic, along with the equally terrific Modern*
*Pastry just across the street and down a block.*

would cause an oil spill. I carried my brown bag in the same hand that held on to the overhead rail.

Hey, 90% of the time we brown bagged it. The only thing I liked in the cafeteria was hot dogs and brownies – but now that I think about it my mom would also occasionally chop up some hot dogs and make a frittata; eggs and hot dogs.

We had truly little but never expected that the school would feed us for nothing. We had loving parents and grandparents who loved us and made sure that we were well fed. You can keep your Betty Crocker; we had our moms who would send us off with the Italian Good Seal of Approval - the olive oil stain on the bottom of the brown lunch bag.

# A North End Icon:
## D'Alessandro's Religious Goods Store
### By Anthony D. Cortese

Across the street from the North Bennet Street Industrial School, and close to the once very active corner of Salem and Sheafe Streets, was **D'Alessandro's Religious Goods Store at # 44 North Bennet Street.**

The two-room store on the street floor of a tenement type building was called by North End residents **"The Saint Store,"** for reasons you can guess by looking at the image **(Figure 1: Image of the Saint Store.).** It was founded by my maternal grandmother, Nonna Lucia D'Alessandro, in 1927 about 15 years after she immigrated from Avelino, Italy and married Silvio D'Alessandro from Foggia. It was taken over by my Aunt Helen (Elena D'Alessandro) in 1961 after Nonna Lucia died. It was closed in 1999 after serving the North End community for 72 years.

The Saint Store specialized in religious goods, such as statues, bilingual bibles, chalices, crucifixes, priests' vestments, Italian and English greeting cards and rosaries. The store also collected clothes and money annually for the Franciscan Mission in Tegucigalpa, Honduras, which was founded and led by Nonna Lucia's brother, Bishop Bernardine Mazzarella, OFM, who was the first principal of Christopher Columbus High School. Nonna Lucia's son, Fr. Francis D'Alessandro, OFM, taught Latin Greek and Hebrew in the seminaries of The Franciscan Immaculate Conception Province (NY and NE.). It was an obvious business for my family to be involved in, especially given the needs of immigrants mostly from the impoverished area of Southern Italy and Sicily.

Not surprisingly, there was a large extended family living in the 4 apartments in the building above the store: my mother and father and four children, two aunts and uncles and their children, Nonna Lucia, Nonno Silvio and Aunt Helen. Several of us were involved in the store in one way or another without formal pay. We didn't expect anything - after all, it was a family business oriented to helping the community. It was spiritually and culturally connected to St. Leonard Church which was down the street and was built by Italian immigrants in 1873. It was the first Franciscan Italian church in New England.

It was a social gathering place for the family, many friends and priests from St. Leonard Church and Christopher Columbus High School. They would wander into the room in the back of the store for coffee and a treat or an occasional quick lunch. It is where Nonna Lucia cooked dinner over a wood/coal and later gas stove for 6-8 of us many days of the week. Later my mother Cecilia took over the role. Many store customers loved coming in to experience the aroma of gravy, stews, even tripe at times, that wafted into the store through the open door. The back room was also the place we cooked for big family gatherings on a Sunday or a holiday when the store was closed. The bench was the place to dry the homemade pasta or the ravioli. The meals were upstairs in one of the apartments with the table often extending through two rooms. Relatives from out of town would often join the feast. My siblings and I loved to bring friends from high school and college who never experienced one of those classic 3-hour Italian Sunday dinners with the multiple animated conversations. We always warned our friends to pace themselves through a multi-course meal, especially because our mother would encourage seconds at every course. The friends never listened to us, but theyhad a great time and still reminisce about it to this day!

**The Broad Role in the North End Community**

The Saint Store was iconic in the community, for a number of reasons. Nonna Lucia, and later, my Aunt Helen and my mother, Cecilia, helped many North Enders that were not literate in Italian and/or English. They provided translations of bills and government documents, and wrote and translated letters to and from Italy for residents corresponding with their families in Italy. Of course, they had the necessary stamps. They also helped North Enders select greeting cards for all occasions in English and/or Italian from the store's interesting collection. They wrote notes, stamped them and my sisters, Palma and Lucille (who also helped with writing) the took them to be posted. Nonna Lucia was beloved in the community.

It was customary to have certain types of religious items donated to the Catholic churches engraved with the name of the families making the donations, e.g., chalices, ciboria, communion plates, and cruets. The store provided this service through Patrick Marino & Sons, jewelers in the Jewelers building across from Filene's Dept. Store. Once we were old enough, my siblings and I took over the job as couriers.

The religious society feasts were a big deal for the store. In addition to providing the 2-4 foot long religious candles that many society members carried during the processions, they were open during the feasts for some of the needs they could supply for the participants. The Sunday processions would often stop at the store for a rest before turning the corner on Salem Street to head up to Charter Street. I often wondered why they did that until I learned that my father, Nick, would sometimes bring some of the men carrying the statue a little refreshment!

My father, Nick, and Uncle Frank, (along with us kids) acted as the delivery service for statues. There were many trips to New England Statuary Co. on Albany Street, South Boston and then to the customers in the North End, East Boston, Medford, Somerville, Revere. We can still remember the dust and the smell of paint at the factory. The Arthur Amadei family who owned the factory became good friends of the family.

**The cultural and spiritual impact of the Store**

The tiny store had an interesting cultural impact. Many of my friends and those of my sisters, brother Nick and cousin Frances told us stories of how they felt when they entered the store.

Some said they thought they should genuflect before a crucifix, or a statue of Jesus or Mary. Some said the regretted that they weren't as good Catholics as they thought they should be after viewing the statues. Some said that entering the store made them realize they should go to confession when they left. Others said they felt like it was helping make connections to some of their better aspirations. Others said they dreaded going in because, somehow, they would be outed for bad behavior!

North Ender and BU professor, Dr. Jimmy Pasto provides some interesting perspective in Anthony Riccio's last book: "<u>Stories, Streets, and Saints: Photographs and Oral Histories from Boston's North End</u>." (2023)

"I used to go by the store every day on my way to or from St. Anthony's school. I went in often, alone or with my friends, to look at the model airplanes and ships and to look at the statues of the saints and read their stories. The store itself felt like it was a kind of sacred space, and a very safe and protective one. I can explain this better if you know what the saints were to us. First, they were our superheroes: powerful beings we could call on for aid with any problem from serious illness to lost objects. We usually did so through someone who had a special connection to the saint. For my family, that person was Aunt Connie. If you lost an important item and needed to find it, you asked Aunt Connie to say a prayer to Saint Anthony. Once she did, you knew the object would turn up--it always did. Of course, we understood that it was the power of God who was revealing the object. The saint simply gave our request a jump up to the ear of God, while my Aunt Connie was there to pass it to the saint. It was all about connections. As for the image of the saint, we saw it as symbol, like the photograph of a relative--an ever-comforting reminder, tangible and accessible, of the protection of the saint. 'This was especially important for people like us who really had little actual power of our own as weighed against forces of the world.

Second, the saints were "characters," individuals marked by certain idiosyncratic features, larger-than-life personality, a certain look, a remarkable life story, or all these factors together. Characters, as Brian Culkin says, give "an extra sense of life" to local life "through their simple, but remarkable, presence." Characters signify as an individual "that the neighborhood socially produced." Characters are therefore inseparable from the neighborhood as a whole: its location, history, ethnic makeup, and social organization.

The saints were remarkable presences to us by virtue of their miraculous deeds but also because of their remarkable lives and personalities, which included the kinds of faults, quirks, and struggles that we knew in ourselves. Their lives were inseparable from our own, and we celebrated them not only in private devotion and calls for help but also in our feasts, processions, church rituals and saints' day celebrations. Just like the saints in the window of the store, we also had living superheroes. 'They were not Superman or Wonder Woman but rather our parents and grandparents, our coaches and community leaders, a fantastic ball player or street fighter, an incredibly kind woman--or an incredibly beautiful one, a renowned lover, a talented singer. Their fame did not go much beyond the neighborhood, but that was enough. The neighborhood was where it was at. We know who they were."

**Transition of the Store over Time**

As we know, no community, its members or its institutions remains the same over time. Given the population explosion and economic, cultural, and political changes in society during the 40's, 50's and 60's the store had to adapt. The market for religious goods began to peak as the population of children began to explode. The North End saw the rapid growth of its elementary, junior high and high schools – 1 public and 4 Catholic elementary schools, a public junior high school and 2 Catholic high schools in this crowded area of less than a square mile. The demand for school supplies was high and the "Saints' Store stepped up to provide some of them.

At the same time kids in the neighborhood sought toys, other playthings, and of course, candy! Again, the Saints' Store responded under the leadership of Aunt Helen D'Alessandro (Figure 2: Image of Aunt Helen.) The list was long. Marbles to play with on gas, water and electricity metal covers on the street. Topps baseball cards with a thin slab of chewing gum in the package – essential for boys to trade and play pitch to win from their rivals. Balsa model airplane kits. Spinning tops. Yo-yo's. Rubber balls filled with air – pimple balls, star balls - essential for handball, "errors", punch ball, stick ball. Pimple balls were the favored type and hard to get. The store had a good supply. (My friends often asked if I could get a free ball - even at 10 cents it was expensive in the 50's.) Wiffle balls and bats. Plastic jewelry. Miniature plastic dinosaurs. I could fill a page with the trinkets. Many were displayed on the top of glass display cases for the religious goods and at the feet of one of the statues. Picture a dinosaur at the foot of St. Francis! It was quite comical. Occasionally, a controversy would occur. I was there when a middle-aged man from Cooper Street came into the store to berate my Aunt Helen for selling water guns because they were causing kids to catch cold. There was no backing down for her!

Where did Aunt Helen get all this tchatchke (as my Jewish friends would aptly call it?) From wholesalers in the dwindling and rundown buildings off Hanover Street on the other side off the elevated Central Artery (Southeast Expressway) near the old Scollay Square. Places like House of Hurwitz (which still exists online, thanks to research by Nick Dello Russo.) As kids, my three siblings, Cousin Frances and I would walk up to the wholesalers and carry the goods back – mostly in small enough quantities to make it work (the boxes of marbles were some-times a challenge.) We walked under the expressway which was a large dingy open air parking lot, through a walkway and short tunnel with lots of aromas from dogs, cats, and temporary human residents. Of course, Aunt Helen would give us treats.

Like many other experiences of many North End families, it was not always easy for the Saint Store and our larger family. An old building needing constant repairs, very small space in the store, the storerooms and the apartments. No running hot water until I was 7 years old (baths at the bathhouse down the street – now the Nazzaro Center.) But it was home for us, and it taught us the important lessons: individual hard work, respect and loyalty to family, caring about the well-being of the entire North End community and beyond, gratitude to our forebears who took the arduous journey to come to America, became active, loyal citizens and helped build and defend the American culture. Of course, great gratitude to the Catholic and other places of worship that helped shaped our values and build our community from the very beginning. The Saint Store and my family are grateful to be a part of this important story.

Acknowledgements

Thank you to my siblings, Palma Cortese, Lucille Cortese Prawdzik and Nick Cortese, and my cousin Fran Bechtold, who lived in our building and was like a sister to us. Their memories, anecdotes and enthusiasm make our lives so rich and made this story possible. Thanks also to Dr. James Pasto for his section of the story and to all my friends from the Friends of the North End who gave me so many fond memories of their experience with the Saint Store.

D'Alessandro's Religious Goods Store, known in the neighborhood as
"the saint store," 44 North Bennet Street, 1982.

Elena D'Alessandro, owner of her religious goods store,
44 North Bennet Street, 1982.

# Religious Store
## By Nick Dello Russo

*This is an email that Nicky Dello Russo sent to his friend Tony Cortese..*

"Tony, I remember your family's religious store very well because it was right across the street from Shaw House. It was one of several religious goods shops in the North End. I remember your aunt had a photo of Bishop Mazzarella on the wall keeping an eye on things. The bishop visited Columbus High School when I was a student there and all the priests made a big deal about him.

I remember buying a scapular in their shop. It was a kind of Catholic necklace made of cloth with two opposing images. One side, which was worn on the chest, had the Sacred Heart of Jesus. The other side, worn on the back, had the Virgin Mary. We were told that wearing a scapular would protect the wearer from going to hell no matter how bad they were. That sounded like a pretty good insurance policy especially know-ing the kind of stuff that went on in my father's barroom. I wore one for a couple of years but it irritated my skin and you couldn't go swimming with it on.

The other things I was fascinated with were the saint's relics they sold. Those were called third class relics and were small pieces of cloth that had touched a first, a piece of the saint's body, or second, something a saint owned, class relic. It all seemed so mystical. I saved up to buy a few relics thinking the saints would protect me from an early death. See, it worked.

Some of the rosaries and crucifixes were also considered third class relics but those were expensive.

The biggest North End religious goods store was the Helio Light Company on Hanover Street. It was where Mike's pastry

140

shop is now located. They specialized in candles of all sizes and a multitude of religious statues. I loved the one of Jesus which was a concave sculpture. As you walked by the eyes would follow you. How creepy was that? I think there was a similar one of Mary but never one of Joseph. I always wondered why we talked endlessly about the Virgin Mary but never about the Virgin Joseph. If Mary was a Virgin he must have been one as well. True?

One of my friends lived on North Margin Street right next to John & Mary's candy store. His grandmother lived upstairs and had a statue of the Infant of Prague in her apartment. The statue depicted baby Jesus and was enclosed in a glass coffin with votive candles spread out in front.

The statue was dressed in vestments whose colors would change in concordance with the liturgical calendar. The candle glass holders would have similar colors, green for ordinary time, white for Easter and Christmas, rose for Gaudate and Laetare Sunday, etc. I thought that was so cool, kind of like a Catholic Barbie doll collection.

My friends and I had a candle club. We would buy some candles at one of the religious shops and sneak into cellars of North End buildings. We'd look for buildings that a back door or window that led into the cellar and if the cellar had some wine barrels that was a bonus. Lots of buildings had rats which was a problem but sampling home made wine was fun.

Religious goods are still popular but are sold mostly on line. I miss going into a shop filled with statues, candles, medals, chalices and all kinds of holy objects. Jesus' eyes would follow you as you walked around making sure you didn't forget to pay for anything but if you did, the scapular would protect you.

Life in the North End was so interesting and so much fun."

# North End Nicknames
## By Victor Passacantilli

It was a beautiful Spring Saturday afternoon in 1959 and I decided to go for a walk.

I exited my apartment on Hanover Street and started walking toward the Prado

I stopped in the Boston I Grocery Store to say hello to Buster and Muffy before buying some penny candy in Charlie Buick's.

As I crossed over Charter Street I waived to Johnny Shoes, Joe Shoes and Frankie Shoes across the way who were talking to Tony Chisel, the Green Man, Bobby the Greaser and Gunga Din.

As I approached the Fire House I stopped to say hello to Ten Minutes to Two who was sitting comfortably in front chatting with Pete the Plank and Charlie Peg Leg.

The Prado is always busy on Saturdays and sure enough Spinny Moe, the Hawk and Slap the Base were playing 3 card poker on a bench.

And with any card game in the North End there are always the kibitzers standing over each player watching intently as the players squeezed out their cards; when The Hawk squeezed out the Queen of Spades to fill his Ace high flush, Wee let out a screech that gave the hand away.

I lost interest quickly with the game and crossed the street to go to confession in Saint Stephen's Church where I bumped into Dom Di Magg coming out of the confessional. He appeared at peace as he knelt next to Billy Bong and his brother, the Blur who were doing their penance.

I stopped in Green Cross Pharmacy and ran into Mikey Moose who was helping Gaggles and Quack Quack find the Brioschi.

I crossed the street to enter Frank's Restaurant and had a drink at the bar with Benny Boy, Dunbar and C.C.

My next stop was at Baby's Pool Room. Saturdays was always a busy day there as one would expect. A lot of the regulars were present: Tony Jay, Cuz, Boom Boom, Blubber, Blouser Mike, Big Sid, Georgie Hats, the Biffer, Dasher, Billy Hagen, Jimmy Wild, Floppy, Ernie the Gasher, Jesse James, Willie Aggie, Fuzzy, Guy Dirt, Mr. Clean, Cry Baby, Huck, Pat the Jew, Abigail, Aggie, Johnny Cucks, Larry Lumps, Louie the Muzzler, Maguire, Magee, Maggie, Magaygen, Buzz Buzz, Nasty Pete, Paulie Hook, Big Head, Allie Goo, Bernie Bell,Bone Head, Smigsy, Benny the Blood, Big Al, Skinny Al, Fat Nick, Skinny Nick, Sick Nick, Bidda Bip, Spunky Joe, Static in the Attic, Scuzzie, Viggy, Black Bart, Weave, Wizzy, Yacky, Yima, Yumpy, Zanga, Zeetha, Ziggy, and Zimmy!

I decided to leave when Dead Eye and Dan the Mugger started arguing over the Red Sox and Yankee rivalry and who was better Joe Di Magg or the Splendid Splinter. I listened for a while finally realizing that this debate will endure forever in the North End.

My next stop was at Burden's Pharmacy. As I entered, I spied Drill the Hole, Jake the Bloke and Cueball being served a Tamarindo by Melon Head at the counter. I said hello to Champie before leaving.

I crossed the street to go to Fiore Christy's Smoke Shop to get a Boston Herald. I went in and ran into the Boccie who was playing his numbers with Wimpy. I preferred to play my numbers with Billy Bus.

I started my trek back home when I was greeted by Herman the German, Tony in the Yard and the Caveman in front of the Circle Pizza which was owned and operated by brothers: Faw Faw, Baba and Lindell.

Then in front of Saint Stephen's Church I witnessed the North End Girls' Choir rehearsing. Bubbles, Palmy Red, Chinzi, Ju Ju, Bunnie, Tootsie, the Plant Lady, Jeannie the Bear, and Josie

Stu Stu were singing mellifluously. Kudos are in order for choirmasters: Suzie Black and Anna Gun.

I approached 422 Hanover Street contented and energized by my friends, my neighbors and the percolating magical vibe the North End is constantly exuding.

One more stop in the Blue Front Restaurant before I went upstairs. My dad, Al Blue Front and my uncle Curly were tending the bar serving the many locals who find almost anything they need outside of their homes: a drink served at the bar, a meal prepared by Maranda, a number to play with Jay Jay Spaceman, a horse to bet with Joe Pips, a card game to be played with Benny Check, DoDo Check, AirOplane Red, Wally Mambo and Mambo Nick and friends to commiserate with. Also, sitting in a booth were Sonny Ash Can, Cocky Blue, Cocky Ross and Jimmy Spats who were mocking Brother Ben, Brother Bill and Engine Joe who were reading the Racing Form in the adjacent booth trying to pick a winner in the 5th race at "Suffering Downs."

Just then a Boss and Under drinking game broke out amongst 6 friends: Itchy Man, Mop Head, Salami Morta, Boopsie, Marly the Ghost and Joe Head.

It got so competitive and boisterous that Blind Nick had to step in to referee the disputes.

My Saturday walk on "my magical island" has come to an end for this time. Next time I hope I run into: Yemma, Peaches, Fingers, Bee Bop, Topper, and Sabu. I missed them today.

## A REMINDER

The North End Athletic Association will sponsor its football league championship later this year. There are 3 teams left in the tournament:

The North End Foodies and The North End Os will play to determine who will face the Zoo in the championship game.

All proceeds will go to renovating the ''Gassie Playground,"

"The Marble Yard" and "The Barges."

| Roster: NE Foodies: | Roster: NE Os : | Roster: The Zoo |
|---|---|---|
| Coach, Taffy Mouse | Coach, Seymo | Coach, Billy |
| PLAYERS: | PLAYERS: | PLAYERS: |
| Mangia Mangia | Anko | Billy the Bug |
| Joe Bananas | Biffo | Beaver |
| Joe Cheese | Bucko | Bison Head |
| Joe the Clam | Cleeko | Canary |
| Joe Crabs | Chimbo | Frankie Fly |
| Joe Beans | Cigelo | Frankie Flea |
| Joe Buns | Eskimo | Hawkeye |
| Joe Bag of Donuts | Guso | Joe the Horse |
| Cabbage | Flippo | Joe Cat |
| Charlie Foonj | Jimbo | Joe the Owl |
| Fish Cake | Jumbo | Joe Giraffe |
| Gizzard | Jocko | Joe Gorilla |
| Guy Beans | Hippo | Joe Wolf |
| Junior Hot Dog | Lippo | Jay Bird |
| Frankie Hot Dog | Lappo | Jack Ass |
| Fudgy | Lobo | John the Bear |
| Johnny Pie | Primo | Bull Dog |
| Salami Morta | Pipinello | Leo the Lion |
| Lemon Lou | Rino | Pat the Rat |
| Lenny Quahog | Trippo | Rabbit |

145

| PLAYERS: | PLAYERS: | PLAYERS: |
|---|---|---|
| Malazza Beans Horse | Tonto | Ronnie Rocking |
| Meatball Gus | Warpo | Snake |
| Vinny Quahog SeaDog and | YoYo Babaloo and | Snakey Puma and |
| Soupy | Jimmy Bow | Hippo |

May the best team win.

My Personal Oz
By Howard Dinin

## Not Quite Kansas

It's very hard to remember details from that time of my life, so little turns out to be worth remembering. That is, there's so little I remember, and certainly not details. There was a novelist, Virginia Woolf in fact, who remembered long periods of her life as being filled with "non-being." It would be nice, and fitting, if it were someone like Giuseppe di Lampedusa or Italo Calvino, but no. She called it a large amount of "cotton wool," with week after week passing and nothing making an impression on her, not a "dint." That was pretty much my life back then.

It's not a wonder, looking back nearly 50 years. Still a very young man, I had, all the same, experienced my share of numbing life circumstances. They starred a wayward wife, forcing me to live by myself in our house in the country, in Ipswich—real small-town New England. And I, I was still largely shaped by my big city existence and ways.

Our house was a rickety farmhouse from the 19th century, right in the center of town, on quite a bit of land. We had just begun to make it habitable again, also less unsightly, less dilapidated, when she took off "to figure out things." This mission required removing herself to another town. Funded by an opportune promotion at her job, requiring training at the corporate mother ship, she packed up for New York.

Her displacement was the first "sudden violent shock," as V. Woolf called it, to penetrate the cotton wool of a sleepy, maybe even a stupefied, existence for me by then. It was brief. I lapsed into that state of non-being that got me through each day, so much like the one before, and the one following.

"You're the one who wants to be separated. You should see a lawyer. Begin divorce proceedings. I'm not the one who left. It's not me who wants to be divorced."

"I can't deal with it. I can't do it. You'll have to."

I did. I presented her with the preliminary papers on Christmas Day, 1976, for which she had returned home, in a ceremonial and purely fictitious acknowledgment of our standing as a household and an institution. That it also marked the bicentennial anniversary of the most consequential year in the history of our country went entirely unnoticed by us.

I served her the papers in a gift box also containing a grey t-shirt emblazoned with the word "HARVARD" in blocky crimson letters, and a small, exquisite (if I say so myself) pin in the form of a fly, set with diamond chips, from Shreve Crump & Low, the jewelers, the Tiffany's of Boston. Each gift carried a meaning. The t-shirt was my way of telling her I was Harvard material, having been accepted in the Graduate School with Special Student status for as long as I could pay the tuition. The gilt and bedizened winged pest, I thought, was self-explanatory. The papers were her gift to herself, me as agent. One not willing, but the actor, the other the opposite. Whatever the layers of ambivalence, the act was played.

The years of living cocooned in cotton wool began. Two years passed, season to season, unremarkably, indistinguishable to me in retrospect. In memory the days, summer and winter, had the quality of lying in a meadow under a blue sky, with the soft drone of the ambient summer sounds, no staccato beats, no rumbles, just a soft near-hum, a whoosh, muffled and, for the moment, eternal-seeming. Cotton wool. They were the two years of our divorce negotiations.

They ended abruptly.

**The House Lands**

Instead of the house landing on the witchy woman, it landed on me. She was on the inside, looking out, by a series of strokes of the hand of a god who was in a particularly ironical mood.

I was on the outside, no longer interested in what was within, its full weight spiritually pressing on me. And no ruby slippers.

The witchy woman ended up owning the farmhouse. And by order of our agreement, throwing me out, with a one-month deadline.

My first task was to extricate myself. Yet, I preferred cocooning where I found myself, and I did nothing about moving my person, never mind all my belongings. I did nothing until three days before the date on which a judge had put his seal, in early summer.

The crab grass and dandelions were already emerging on what had been, to the embarrassment of our neighbors, what we called the "south 40" and they thought should be a lawn.

## The Red and the Green

I ended up on a street of what might as well have been a mystical land. I'd say, a land of imagination and the exotic. But it was real enough. Not Oz exactly but close, very close. A kind of Oz. A place replete with what were to me bands of odd inhabitants, welcome eventually to my presence or just as strangely indifferent to it.

The street was Moon Street, two short blocks long, between North Square and Fleet Street, and I would append the usual North End Homeric epithet "historic." I would, except, as far as I can gather, especially in terms of importance to anyone but me, not much of significance is chronicled about this tiny byway, except for my arrival on it. Prior to the nineteenth century, from the cartographic evidence it did not exist.

How did I know I was in a different milieu?

The fact impinged on my consciousness for the first time on the exact day I moved in. I had taken the place sight unseen; thanks to the intervention of friends I had barely realized were that close. I first appreciated their genuine well-meaning only later. I had remained in the proverbial dark until pulling up at the curb.

While moving a houseful of furniture up two flights to my walk-up on a street that, until three days before, I hadn't been aware existed, I noticed the somber walnut patina of the paneling had seams that had been mechanically painted on. The detail did not require too close inspection. The wood was everywhere, on the stairways and stairwells, on the walls of every room but the kitchen and bathroom. On the floors, a note of decor, the only break in the coffered confines, was a still intact, though not new, tangled looking shag carpet, wall to wall. It was a blend of crimson and darker fibers, not wool, not cotton, clearly durable.

But the main stimulant to the violent re-awakening of consciousness, the rude stripping away of my cotton wool cocoon, was the kitchen. It was unremarkable in most regards, graduate student grade appliances. The wall color was a somewhat offbeat choice. Not an emerald-green, suitable to the jolly old land of Oz. It was very dark green and still had a sheen that hinted at the gloss when new.

But the horse of a different color—not an odd color at all, but with a certain suitability for its function, even expected—was the main feature in my shock surveying the fittings and conveniences of the room.

There, amid a cooking range, a sink, space for a table and chairs—the focus of the cupboards surrounding it all—was a full-size claw-footed porcelain bathtub. I saw it, and ancient stirrings of my blood inherited from my immigrant forebears began to hum.

## Ch-ch-ch-changes

These spare vestiges of tenement life were subliminal reminders that "my people," as I only half-jokingly referred to the prior wave of immigrants on these teeming streets, were closely related existentially. The narrow, crooked streets, following colonial cow paths to hilly pastures, once had echoed to the diphthongs, nasality, and guttural Germanics of Yiddish, my

153

antecedents' lingua franca, where, by 1979, they now rang with the broad-a and missing "r" of a native Bostonian, inflected with the frequent addition of Italian slang epithets.

When I was introduced to the North End, I was just another college student, an Anglo (though as a self-consciously Jewish "other" all my life, I had been given enough cues in the native Bronx of my first years to know, somehow, I was the "other").

The North End was exclusively Italian, or Italo- as some would style it, by any virtual census, since decades before my pale yid face began to haunt those streets. It was already evident, especially to my hyper-academic sensitization, that the North End was in a kind of stasis. It was what James Joyce, speaking of 1904 Dublin, dubbed a paralysis, wherein Dubliners found themselves frozen, or locked in the amber of a bygone time, from some time in the late 18th century, even down to the way they transfigured the English they spoke and to the shape of their quotidian.

I had grown up to stories of my immigrant family and the way of things on the Lower East Side of New York, where the great steamships had dumped them 50 years before the days recalled in this reminiscence—a full hundred years ago. But by some magic, in the here and now, in the 70s North End, life seemed to pass in an endless span of heedless days and nights, with the pace and allure of a set way of life. The greatest enchantment was the abiding predictability as one day slid into the next, and the greatest preoccupations were still somehow to earn and to pay, in coin, what was demanded for the shelter and comfort of what can only be called an enduring reassuring hubbub, a per-petual repetition of sameness. Oh, and to wonder, what would be the meat in that week's gravy?

But as I say, in the way of a Woolfian "violent shock" of one moment—and then another—for me, change was afoot. And I was very aware of it, forced as I was to vigilance. But they didn't come about in my routine.

154

Somehow, I had implanted myself in one of the few remaining, largely untouched storied brilliantly colorful ways of life deep in the heart of a sprawling web of urban renewal and revitalization. It was now where I lived, but not my home, if it would ever be. As for the clangorous disruptive reality of "out there," on the other side of the Artery, none of it touched the lives of my new neighbors as far as I could tell. In time, in 50 years afterward, I learned it never would, even as the inhabitants melted away, usually to life beyond this one, sometimes to the suburbs, never forgetting where their hearts continued to beat at the same synchronized pulse as their dearest friends had been for a lifetime.

Though not part of it—I was never invited by a neighbor, doors or streets away, to dinner—I was not oblivious to it. To become part of the life, you had to accept, like falling in love without doubt, or submitting to a rite or ceremony or a long list of what I'll call secular sacraments. From boosting a ride in a "cousin's" car, to going with a nervous friend to the navy recruiter; all are necessary if not compulsory customs in this true enclave.

The real natives had the true homie court advantage. Somehow, maybe silently, by some Anglo body language, because I never sought them out, I was never sought to be in. Maybe, at 33, I was already too old, and known to be unreceptive to join in when the lindy hop began.

The way of life in the North End, as close as a walk down the block, or a peek at that tub in the kitchen, was at once remarkable, to me, and familiar to everyone else. Not a thought given to it; cotton wool. It was familiar, after more than ten years as a guest, but perhaps in the way of an anthropologist on repeated field trips among the indigenous species.

What was strange was the disruption in my life. Yet I was surrounded by people to whom a quick break at the Caffe Graffiti for a quick espress' or a more leisurely cortado, was as routine as a saunter for me to Harvard Square for a two hour dally over a mug of the featured varietal at Coffee Connection. As in so many aspects of daily and weekly household management, I never succumbed to the local ways.

It was time to face the strange. Not that the North End was entirely strange. I had in the dozen years since college become a habitué of certain streets along the waterfront. More particularly, specific venues were regular haunts, especially since my days of an involuntary semi-bachelorhood.

In some ways there was no better place than the North End to return, seemingly, to a way of life I had abandoned—perhaps a turn or two of the dial past "10" than was advisable—when I married. That act had begun the decade, and this one closed it.

At the time, I had no sense of such a culmination. My workplace remained mere blocks away to the east, in the deep shadows of the brutal design of the multitudinous trestles of the Central Artery, tracing the rim of abandoned wharves and docks, the decayed glory of a critical part of the founding and growth of our country. But for now, these remained the orphaned fringes of what had been and was only just reawakening.

The North End is the nexus of changes in the history of Boston. What had been the densely inhabited heart of a vital colonial port, which became downtown, slowly was expanded with massive landfills—scrapings hauled by the truckload from the Blue Hills and part of Beacon Hill. These predated the creation of the Back Bay neighborhood started toward the end of the 19th century, the final stage of the transformation of that bulbous peninsula into the city we know in the present.

However, during my brief settlement, told here, in the North End, the modernization had barely begun with the revitalization of the waterfront, just two blocks from my new front door. Two blocks in the other direction and I could find myself—unfortunately only in the literal sense—on Hanover Street.

Fifty years ago, as even until now, Hanover Street was the emblematic main artery of the fabled Italian North End. There is very little sign remaining, though, that when it was named it originated at the base of Beacon Hill. The street was designated on a map entitled "A New and Correct PLAN of the TOwN of BOSTON And PROViNCiAL CAMP."

The artifact was commissioned as an engraving and published by "Pennsylvania" magazine of Philadelphia in 1775. The street's origins were erased, no doubt indefinitely, some time before the North End was dissected from the rest of town when the demolition and construction for the Central Artery within a decade bifurcated or entirely obliterated several neighborhoods that had taken centuries to form.

With the chief beneficiary being my own understanding, given that it's embedded in a fanciful imagination, I believe that with the machinations of the city, state, and the federal government despite the physical disconnection from the vitality and ingrained historical importance of the North End, they left it largely intact. It was a kind of tacit encouragement to the good citizenry to preserve and reinforce an innate sense of self-preservation.

It was permission to a people who never asked for it to turn their backs on a city that knew only one kind of pride and begrudged respect to any but their own. North Enders were a breed apart; their insularity, chauvinism, and independence allowed survival of the problems of life. Even with a population that included an enduring percentage of stalwarts who responsively turned their backs to the Anglos, and managed to thrive speaking only their native Italian, and little or no English.

157

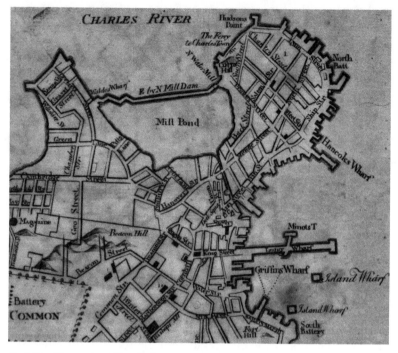

*Public Domain, The Library of Congress*

## Sh-boom and Fo Shizzle

Fortunately for me, my new home on Moon Street was itself in a period of transition—with no sense of it in the minds of any of the players in my little drama of life changes. Clearly, in retrospect, it had been modernized, though with intact vestiges of the sociological artifacts of past tenement life—enough to ensure my sense of the high level of "character" of my dwelling: a Hobson's choice I had ginned up out of my own anxiety and inaction. I had had no choice. Nevertheless, I felt a faint affection for it, perhaps because I heard the chords of memory of my own humbler beginnings in a rent-stabilized apartment in the post-War 40s.

Once the rental truck was unloaded, I gave myself not a moment to settle in. I had walked up and down those narrow stairs too many times, a standard feature of housing ultimately designed to house as many people as possible as could be fit into as little space as could be offered to people only a few steps above penury.

I myself of course was not penurious or even close, despite the economic beating I took by electing precipitously to end the divorce negotiations with the other side. My emotional state had withered in two years of wrangling and the preposterous legal postures my ex-wife's lawyer had cooked up to try to trip me up. Rather they wore me out, and the effect was the same.

I looked at the many many cartons of unpacked belongings that filled every one of the four rooms of my "cave." And I could not face a weekend, all alone, in a sudden wave of stifling weather for a summer in Boston that was just revving up. I had visions of myself, a true Melvillian isolato, dark-browed in my garret, just under the eaves of a forgotten tenement just a moment's stumble from the decayed wharves of an old New England port that tended to forget such as me.

Whatever my romantic notions about my plight, I was lonely and needed company. It wouldn't take a Freud to figure out my next move. I called a former teaching colleague, a friend who knew me from the past, a past that included a mutual familiarity with the college where we had been teaching and where I met the young woman who became my future ex-wife. I called out of the blue, not entirely characteristic of me.

Tom's wife answered the phone and handed me off to him, who said "Sure, come on up! We'll find something to drink…" It was that weekend, when, too far gone to drive back the two hours from New London, New Hampshire, to the sweaty streets of the North End, I was invited to stay overnight Friday, and then another night, when the dinner guest was a new colleague of my friend's wife at the college. It was the same college at which I had met the wife who had just shed me. Tom's wife told Lucy, "Pay no attention to our friend, he's just an old drinking friend of Tom's; we can do better than him." In two years, Lucy and I were married, and moving from that third floor walk up to a rent-controlled apartment in Brookline.

I was fated to live parts of my life all over again, jumping from what I had thought was the fire, but not far enough, and landing in the skillet. Not as bad, but hot enough to burn.

I should have stayed in the North End, and gone to the European Restaurant, on Hanover Street, one of the go-to places for going on 50 years where families gathered and celebrated for the smallest reason. And I should have had at least one bottle of chianti and introduced myself to the nearest table of celebrants. But I didn't.

I went to a small New England Yankee town for a return engagement—so to speak—and was infatuated by a clone of the recently player vacated vacated from the role of helpmate. Not only no help, but blind to it by my hopelessness.

The North End for all its purely surface simplicity and lack of grace, was innately a place of hope. It had been for hundreds of thousands of very poor people for over a hundred fifty years, who rose above their apparent fate and made a heaven from its rough streets. Doo-wop, one of the arts that rose from similar mean streets, and echoed in the alleys, sang anthems to the hope and vision of paradise that lived in every heart.

> *Life could be a dream, sh-boom*
> *If I could take you up in paradise up above*
> *If you would tell me I'm the only one that you love*
> *Life could be a dream sweetheart.*
> *Hello, hello again*
> *Sh-boom and hoping we'll meet again[1]*

---

1. ©1954, *The Chords: Keyes, Feaster, Feaster, McRae, and Edwards*

In one of many ironies, two years before, when I needed a lawyer, I turned to my friend Dom, a true North End native, and denizen of its streets since his birth.

He referred me to a colleague, a well-known labor lawyer, who recommended the services of a new associate, a woman, who was a legal crackerjack and supremely smart, strategic beyond her years.

The irony arose from their offices fronting on Commercial Street, four or five doors from Dom's restaurant. Though no one could foresee it, least of all me, they were to be, two and a half years hence, just a long block's walk away from my new digs. It was the same walk I mentioned earlier to the newly emerging Waterfront area.

The irony was, as a result of calling a halt to the proceedings, I had divested myself of the need for their services and found myself where I might otherwise have chosen not to be. It was only years later I came to understand the chrysalis stage of a living neighborhood I had unwittingly moved into.

Though just beginning, the North End was in a state of transition, from true native terroir, with its unique gestalt and customs and folkways—and the long rapturous memories of the bliss of growing up there, regardless of circumstance, for the many residents still conducting their lives (in 1979) from its confines—to a kind of living museum, offering the same gustatory experiences it always had to ever-hungry tourists, and the same delicacies and other culinary delights that had been sold to the residents for over a hundred years.

The shops and many of the watering and dining places are still there, even owned and run by the same stalwarts who could not deny their love of "home," but who had long since abandoned the teeming streets for the expanse and comfort of the suburbs.

The apartments and condominiums and cooperative housing—

those newly formulated modes of urban residential living—
were no longer the cramped quarters they had been and had
become precisely the kind of digs meant to appeal to the yuppie
in training I was in danger of becoming.

I remained not only blindered to my own fantasies, but these
also rendered me clueless to the potential redemption of im-
mersing myself in the life of a perfectly vibrant, perfectly vital
neighborhood, at least for what it would teach me about living
in the moment.

The North End took me in. But I turned my back to it.

•

# An Olfactory Journey
## By Dom Capossela

*Can you find the stainless steel bucket that housed the live snails? Find Giuffre's Live Lobsters and look to the right of the entryway.*

*The goal of this display is to help the cook. They place the live snails in that oversized colander and starve them for a few days. This step encourages the snails to expel any remaining food waste from their system.*

*For decades those snails welcomed shoppers to the North End. So old world.*
*Can you smell the fruit and vegetables? Step into that meat market and smell the pain and agony humans inflict on animals. Just kidding. Not pain. Blood and torn flesh.*

*Look at the sign on the top right. Which beer was the 'champagne of bottled beers?*
*Notice the local vendors taking over the street with their fruit and vegetables.*

163

My wife, Toni-Lee, never ordered dinner until she perused the dessert list and saw what indulgence awaited her there. So, taking her example, let's begin our North End olfactory repast with the sweet aromas of the pastry shops.

The cannoli tempt us with their freshly fried, buttery allure, while the lobster tails (the pastry, not the delectable crustacean Italians love made "fra diavolo"), emit a rich blend of butter and vanilla. Sfogliatelle, 'thin leaves', give off a tantalizing hint of caramelization, freshly baked biscotti are redolent with toasted nuts and rich cocoa, and tiramisu adds coffee and cheese to the mix. With a cup of espresso? Come on, we're all Italian.

We had four donut shops in the North End, adding smells of yeast, flour, and sugar, the basics, that combined with the characteristic aromas of the varied additives: cinnamon, vanilla, chocolate, and fruit. Yummy. But all those smells yielded center stage when it came to frying the dough. Whether donut makers were frying beignets, fritters, crullers, churros, or zeppole, the smell of the fry was compelling.

What makes that smell so alluring? Scientists talk the Maillard reaction, they talk lipids and fatty acids, but for me, the smell is simply sugar and caramel conjuring up high-calories and coffee, crunchy exterior and baby-bottom-soft interior. The smell strongly suggests to us to sit, bite, sip, repeat. Indulge, indulge, indulge.

Was bread the anthemic North End smell? One can easily make an argument for it. We had sixteen thriving bakeries, sixteen addresses actively fermenting yeast on premises producing a distinct and tangy scent, something akin to fermenting Champagne. (To produce bubbles in their wine, all Champagne producers add government-regulated yeast to their filled bottles which, besides helping to create the bubbles, produces a signature yeast aroma in that festive libation.)

*Bakers work long and hard and at unusual times. But where would we be without their products? God bless them.*

As the bread bakes, developing a crisp, golden crust, it emits warm, nuanced aromas derived from the lightly caramelized sugars and toasted grains, wheat, rye, or oats, whose flavors run the gamut from earthy to nutty. Certain bread recipes also incorporate spices or herbs like cinnamon, rosemary, or fennel seeds, infusing the bakery with pleasant fragrances that enhance the depth and complexity of the overall aroma.

Coffee culture has always been strong in the North End and cafes are compulsive to us. Besides the stimulating effects of the caffeine, the rich smell of freshly brewed coffee, the company of friends, the quiet buzz of conversation, and the welcome break from routine is invigorating. Each cafe has its own signature bouquet that depends on the pedigree of the coffee used: which variety of bean, from what region, grown at what altitude. Other variables are the processing, the length and heat of the roast, the time expired from the roast to the brewing, and the skills of the barista. All contribute to creating a range of distinct aromas encompassing floral and fruity, nutty and chocolate. Add in the sweet and creamy scent of steamed milk and the aromas of cocoa powder and cinnamon, and you have one of the strong reasons to prefer one café over another: its signature bouquet.

And, on the subject of bread, let's not forget the Italian pizzerias with their scents of baking dough, bubbling cheese, zesty sauce, and various toppings.

*While not nearly as old as the Regina, from the day Paul and Ralph Deuterio opened their iconic thick, cheesy, juicy, scrumptious square pizzas they took their place alongside the Regina as top of the line of their style pizza. And the noontime lines? Well worth the wait.*

*"Salumeria Italiana," a great store. Migno ran it for decades. Guy, his son, carries on. How Italian is it still? Order a half-pound of grated Parmigiana, and they will cut the piece and grind it on the spot.*

Let's step into the enchanting world of the salumerias, where the air dances to an orchestra of delicious scents. The cured meats give off rich, savory aromas interspersed with hints of salt and garlic , black pepper and fennel seeds. The cheeses, like Parmigiano-Reggiano, pecorino, mozzarella, and gorgonzola, have their own unique aromas, ranging from creamy and tangy to nutty or pungent. A selection of olives, both green and black, marinated in herbs like rosemary, thyme, or oregano, and/or spices like fennel seeds and black pepper, in a variety of vinegars and oils, throw out briny and earthy scents. Salumerias were veritable culinary Chanels of fragrances.

167

*This distance photo does a great job illustrating the size and density of the famous Haymarket area, aka Blackstone Street, that hosted vendors who brought marginally-off fresh fruit and produce to people who had to be frugal.*

We had many fresh fruit and produce stores whose seasonal scents became richer and sweeter as the fruit ripened. Bananas, mangoes, peaches and plums, lemons, limes, oranges, and so many others produce rich, zesty, tangy, and refreshing aromas that fill the air.

*Haymarket was synonymous with chaos and disorder. Yelling and screaming were the orders of the day.*

The North End's fish markets were a tribute to the ocean's bounty. They offered a mesmerizing array of seafood, especially to the North Ender whose palate was more sophisticated than the middle-American shopper. Of course the stores carried the well-known and widely popular fish like salmon, tuna, cod, or halibut, or shellfish such as shrimp, lobster, each with its own slightly sweet, briny scent. But in the North End fish markets we also found crabs, squid, octopus, eel, snails, mackerel, and sardines, mostly shunned by mid-America, although over the years many non-Italians did come to appreciate what we found wonderful about less popular varieties.

*Do you believe eight butchers worked in harmony in this tiny space? It was an era when the buyer could be demanding and have her meat cut precisely as she wanted it.*

Blood. With more than a dozen butcher shops, the rich, earthy scent of blood was integral to the neighborhood. We were matter of fact about our food chain. Rather than being turned off by them, we accepted hanging carcasses of venison, rabbits, goats, lamb, and other meats on hooks outside their stores as part of the chain of supply and thought nothing unusual about it. North End butchers catered to their customers. We could ask for especially well-trimmed, for butterflying, cubing, or boning, and the skillful butchers accommodated us with a smile. All

169

hamburger meat was ground when ordered, and butchers made
their own sausages, choosing the right combination of lean
to fat meats, chopping the meat to a desired dice, then adding
their personal trademark blend of spices for which they became
locally famous.

*Safety precautions like keeping meat in a tempera-
ture-controlled, dirt-free, and insect free environment
were often ignored in the North End. There was little
room.*

North End butchers at that time were knowledgeable cooks
who would take the time to help us choose the best cuts of meat
for specific recipes, considering tenderness, flavor, cooking
methods, times, temperatures, seasoning, and, of course, cost.
For them, such personal attention was a labor of love.
Like our fishmongers, our butchers carried meat parts that
middle-America disdained. Because we were good cooks and
had good butchers, we could buy the disdained meats like liver,
kidneys, brains, chicken feet, bone marrow, pig's feet, and
tripe. Oh! My goodness! Our love of tripe was legendary and
persists to this day. Of course, we knew how to best prepare
and cook it. And affordable? Practically given away.

Over time, the butcher got to know what you liked and could
afford. For that reason, every housewife had her own butcher

and wouldn't dream of switching.

Ooops. Sorry. We're supposed to be focused on smells. The most important aroma in a butcher shop was the rich, slightly metallic smell of raw meat and blood, mixed with the rustic smell of the sawdust that covered the floor, and the fresh garlic, herbs, and spices the butcher used for prepared meats. Even the scent of the aging butcher blocks contributed to the distinctive butcher shop bouquet. M'm! M'm! Good!

*Coogie Quahogs was synonymous with selling delicious foods to the North End. Over the decades, he was in innumerable businesses, all successes. The race tracks were delighted with his success: they ended up with the profits.*

Feasts, street festivals, had their own smells. Some pushcarts sold nuts only: almonds, hazelnuts, Indian nuts, or roasted chestnuts, some of the nuts coated in sugar or spices. Some sold briny clams with their lemons and hot sauce. Some, pizza slices. There were grills of sizzling sausages, sweet and spicy, not only with their own aromas of caramelized pork, herbs, and spices, but also the aromas of frying onions and peppers. And who could forget the deep-fryers with arancini (rice balls), fried dough, or zeppole (fried doughnuts), as well as fried seafood with scents of crispy, golden-brown goodness. Pretty amazing.

In the fall came the heady and powerful aromas of wooden barrels and fermenting grapes as many old-timers, aspiring vintners, made their own homemade wine. Although some sold the wine, it was always a labor of love and pride, from the buying of the grapes to the first sips.

My father would hand me an empty quart bottle in a brown bag. I took it to our fruit and vegetable store and went with the owner down to the cellar. We stopped at a very large barrel set on a sturdy shelf at a bit of an elevation. One end of a rubber hose was hidden deep inside the barrel; the other end was tied in a knot handy for the vintner to unravel. He stuck the freed end in his mouth, took a suck of the air out of the hose, and smoothly placed the hose in my empty quart bottle. We watched mesmerized as gravity and the vacuum caused the wine to flow from the barrel into the bottle. The bottle filled, he would pinch the hose and raise it above the level of the wine to stop the flow. A simple knot secured it.

There were other hallmark North End smells, like florists and churches with their candles and incense, but we'll stop here. Our North End was a rich neighborhood, rich in tastes and sounds. Rich in smells.

*The Catholic Churches in the North End were always affiliated with
a grammar school. St. Leonard's was affiliated with St. Anthony's
School. Every religious rite was held here, often with the school
children in enforced attendance.*

*St. Leonard's was the first Church in Boston built to serve the
Italian community. Prior, Roman Catholic Italian churchgoers
suffered a multitude of indignities at the hands of the dominant Irish
population. The Church's bouquet was a simple, lovely combination
of floral, incense, and wax aromas.*

# Restaurants, Luncheonettes, and other Food Shops in the 1950s-60s North End
## *A few for Tourists; a plethora for residents and regulars*

Our North End had about eight full-service restaurants that did a lot of business with tourists.

We had a couple of dozen small breakfast-lunch restaurants that did most of their business with residents or with a regular business clientele.

We had bars that routinely rotated their menu, each night offering patrons a different dinner, standard for that particular night.

Plus, all of the salumerias offered sandwiches to go, (spukies,) and, before work each day, the laborers lined up and waited patiently as the staff worked assiduously to slice the cold cuts and construct the culinary work of art. Despite the time pressure to get to work, that lunch break had to be perfect, so they waited. I can still smell the freshly sliced meats. Italians and food.

Touristy restaurants aside, many of the food shops were also involved in the numbers game, the fairer precursor to the state-run lottery. Fairer, because the boys who operated the numbers game paid out a higher percentage of the take than the state-run lottery does. Of course, who expects the government to be fairer than the rackets? Not I. Besides, you didn't pay taxes when you hit the number. You weren't reported to the IRS. And you could bet as little as a nickel, or even a penny with some bookies who had a heart. The food shops' involvements ranged from actually taking the action to simply providing a comfortable place for regulars to find their regular bookies. And buy a drink or a cup of coffee. After all, we weren't Communists.

## Touring the Early North End Italian Restaurants
### By The Staff

The European was next door to the building my girlfriend grew up in. We would often have our neighborhood Saturday night date there as young teenagers. Chuck, the host, would graciously greet us and show us to a table. Lentil soup and a cheese pizza was a standard order. It was affordable for a the north kid picking up the tab with his earnings as a dishwasher in the Blue Front Restaurant.

*A favorite of college students from across Boston. Stayed open late.*

Giro's was a North End landmark for fine dining. Frankie, the doorman, stayed outside and valeted your car in the crowded neighborhood. Shrimpy, the chef, a master at his craft ruled the kitchen. Frankie jazz stayed at the bar. The waiters, in tuxedos, stayed in the dining room and kept their mouths shut. Maybe, if he was in town, Jimmy Durante, comfortable in this milieu, would come for dinner. Maybe a couple of dignitaries from New York or Rhode Island would stop by to check in from time to time. As for us residents, a well-run, bustling restaurant added some welcome activity to the quiet end of Hanover Street.

*Rumor was that this restaurant was connected.*

Stella's would have a good argument that they were top dog among the better North End restaurants. More celebrities dined there than in any other local restaurant, for example, Cardinal Cushing, Jackie Onassis Kennedy, and Jack Kennedy who, famous for not carrying money, could never find a quarter to tip the valets. The bar was always crowded with distinguished North End dignitaries. The kitchen was staffed by young North Enders eager to gain experience in the art of cooking. And the Polcari brothers carryied on the tradition their family started in

*Stella's served some stars in its day, including Jackie Kennedy. Rumor had it that the Kennedys were poor tippers.*

the restaurant business

The Paul Revere spa on the corner of Hanover and North Bennet Streets was symptomatic of a half-dozen mostly lunch spots geared for residents. It's where I acquired a taste for coffee. Light, no sugar. The owner let us hang out as long as we bought something now and then. It was a haven for us on a cold winter evening with a juke box where we could listen to Beatles hit tunes in the early 60s. Our apartments were too small for our families, so where else are we going to go? Louie and his wife serving Italian peasant dishes, my favorite, Pasta lenticche served piping hot. Don't tell grandma.

Messina's restaurant at the corner of Hanover and Battery Streets was the eponymous work of a wonderful family, hard working people who served decent food and opened at convenient hours. Their clains to fame were one, they served as a hangout for the "coasties" down the street at the United States Coast Guard base. And two, they frequently overserved patrons

177

who often argued, spilling out on Hanover St. to settle their disputes with fisticuffs, providing entertainment for residents who cheered them on from their window sills.

Circle Pizza rivalled the Pizzeria Regina. They were in a prominent location on the corner of Hanover and Fleet Streets, across from the pool room. Often excitement poured out of here that was unfortunately stressful for the family and staff but entertaining for the residents always looking for excitement they were not involved in.

Coogie Quahog came up with the idea of a fried clam and fish place in this Italian restaurant hub. His shop was long and narrow with no seating available. It was affordable for residents and the lines were often long. Great smells. It was a resounding success. Besides the fish, they served deep-fried, oily French fries with a secret sauce of sweet vinegar and red pepper flakes. He used the same sauce when he sold quahogs and cherrystones off the cart. This man was a business and culinary genius, making scads of money.

Perhaps the most popular salumeria for cold cut sandwiches, now long gone, was Iacopucci's. Lines were long, fed not only by the *zappatori*, the construction workers, but also by the nearby high schoolers. Those Italian cold cuts stuffed into the spukies were in high demand for lunch, perhaps half if eaten as breakfast while walking to school. Pick your combination: mortadella, salami, capocollo, provolone cheese and especially prosciutto are often chosen. The counter server snugly embraces the loin of prosciutto in his left arm tucked to his ribs and adroitly slices razor thin pieces with his long carving knife topping his delicate creation with the king of Italian meats. After choosing the meat, add a choice of toppings: cherry hot peppers, a drizzle of virgin olive oil, diced tomatoes or onions perhaps, a distinguished sandwich for North End Italian kids to savor while eating next to their classmates from elsewhere.

For personality, there was no beating Joe the Boss, the explosive force behind Joe Tecce's, creator of Steak Mafia. Joe's food was excellent, the prices were low, and he was a most generous human being. Some say he served after hours, having a small gang of young men at the door to keep the peace. Some say you could get after hours wine there, masquerading as Coca-Cola bottles. Some say Joe the Boss threw bottles now and again.

Last, let's mention the most famous pizza restaurants of the era: Regina Pizzeria and Galleria Umberto. We included comments on each in the captions of their photographs.

We're sorry not to include every food shop. There were many. These will illustrate the selection we did have.

## Restaurant Experience: Louie's
### By Sammy Viscione

North End restaurants were declared off limits in my family. Spending money in restaurants especially on Italian food would be an offense, and a colossal insult to my mother. However, one day I committed that crime.

It happened the nite I returned home after being discharged from military service. Being famished, I , and a friend went to Louie's restaurant on Fleet st. Vito the waiter was a tenant in my building on Sheafe street whom I knew very well. He was glad I was home knowing at the present time the Cuban missile crisis was threatening the world over.

So on , I ordered Louie's signature entrée; vinegar peppers, pork chops and potatoes. Enthusiastically, I relished ever morsel. And because of Vito's munificence it didn't cost me anything so I thought. Subsequently, the price i did pay was the endless time I spent passing that scrumptious dinner while sitting on the throne. Unknowingly, linking a steady regimen of army cooking with an abrupt consumption of Italian food was not gastronomically friendly. Neither was my explanation to my mother.

179

*How Great! Hand printed and featuring Roast Veal (who serves that now?), Pig's Feet, Fried Mushrooms. These people knew how to eat.*

# The Blue Front Restaurant:
## A North End Restaurant and Bar
### By Victor Passacantilli

The Blue Front Restaurant was established by my immigrant paternal grandparents, Mariano and Amaranda Passacantilli in 1933 at 424 Hanover Street. They ran the restaurant/barroom for many years together. It was hard work for both, yet a labor of love. She managed the kitchen and he tended the bar. It was a neighborhood meeting place for locals to stop in for food, drinks and camaraderie with other North Enders. Maranda's skill in preparing home cooked "peasant dishes" was unmatched in the neighborhood. The daily business was brisk and the rewards were lucrative and well earned.

After many years of hard work, it came time to pass the business on to their son, Al and son-in-law, Curly (Florian Fleszar).

*Mama. How we love you!*

Yet, the remaining constant was Maranda. She would prepare the daily menu and serve lunch before retiring for the day. My grandmother's cooking became legendary and is still remembered by many as being the best Italian comfort food. She would serve her Italian specialties like: pastina in brodo, liver and onions, pork chops and vinegar peppers, veal spezzato, polenta, calamari al sugo, fried smelts and verza in podella. Her signature meal was a neighborhood favorite, tripe al sugo served only on Saturdays.

To this day that recipe is fondly recalled by many. I helped her many times to prepare the 30 pounds of tripe. It was truly a painstaking effort but a labor of love for her, not for me, to please her customers. We opened at 11 am and it was all gone by 1 or 2 pm. Neighbors would come to the restaurant with their own pans to get an order or two to take home. Often customers would show up later in the day only to find out that the tripe was sold out.

For lunch on the weekdays, the booths would be filled with workers from The Boston Sausage Meat Company down the street and on the weekends, we would be packed with Boston Edison workers and our regular customers. During the week it was also a favorite spot for cab drivers and the Boston Police to stop in on their lunch or supper breaks.

The Blue Front was also a destination for one to find a book-maker. Bookmakers always needed to be available to their bet-tors and what better place than a restaurant. A place to sit eat, drink and gamble. On any given day you would find more than one bookmaker there. One to play a number with, another to bet a horse or a game. And even a loan shark to borrow from to pay for one's losings. My dad and my uncle did not mind that illegal and pervasive North End activity because it brought in business and the bookmakers were good sports buying drinks and spending money on their customers.

Amongst all that activity were the regulars. They would come by to eat, have a drink, play cards, make a bet, and kibitz. Kib-itzing was an ordinary part of the day. Everyone had a joke to tell, mock someone, make a comment on one's choice of cloth-ing or standing behind someone wincing as a wrong card was played in a game of gin rummy. Every day was the same day in the restaurant as it percolated with all the hustle and bustle.

A truly remarkable and iconic North End establishment.

My dad and uncle worked very hard to continue the cachet that my grandparents strived to establish. Their regime brought the Blue Front to another level as they adjusted to the times.

As the North End started to change and the environs sur-rounding the community and the Government Center became a vibrant area, we noticed our lunch time clientele started to change also. We began to accommodate a more diverse diner. Professionals, City Hall workers, bankers and even assistant district attorneys became regular visitors to the restaurant. Some would return with family and friends for supper. The bookmakers went on guard. People who they did not recognize or look like us were suspected of being "the law." One would ask the bartenders, "chi e questo?" "Who is this?" Then the bartender would give a nod if the customer was okay or shrug if they did not know him/her.

My brothers, Albie, Daniel, Paul, Robert and Mark along with our cousin Eric did our best to shorten the hours Al Blue Front and Curly had to endure. The "store" was open 7 days a week from 8 am until closing which could go late into the evening.

They each worked one week days, one week nights alternating with every other Monday off!!

Although the Blue Front closed in 1983 after 50 years of doing business on Hanover Street, its reputation as an iconic destination for good food, for nurturing lifelong friendships and having a magical ambiance remains alive.

# Vignettes
*A few standalone snapshots highlighting moments unique to the North End.*

## You're Supposed to Know
### By Anthony Coppola as told to Dom Capossela

The daily presence of 'the office', another name for those whose business is not discussed openly, didn't affect the daily lives of most of us growing up in the North End. But, being part of the social fabric of the area, there are things that you're supposed to know, like you didn't raise your hands to someone 'connected.' There's no published list naming those connected: You're supposed to know.

Ever wonder how you learn? How do we know Giro's is 'connected?' You're supposed to know.

So, Anthony is taking his girlfriend out to dinner at Giro's. It's Feb 5, and a major storm is on its way, (turned out to be the Great Blizzard of 1978). The girlfriend asks if her girlfriend could be invited. Big hearted fool that he is, that we all were, he says "Yes." What else do you say to your girlfriend?

In the event, although outside the snowstorm has begun, inside, the restaurant is warm and cozy. Frankie Dinisi, in his stylish tuxedo, is their waiter and comes to take their orders. After Anthony and his girlfriend each orders the reasonably-priced

Chicken Marsala, the friend once-removed orders the most expensive item on the menu, a Lobster Diavolo. To accentuate her rudeness, she orders a side of Spaghetti with Lobster, Shrimp, and Clams. Frankie glances over at Anthony who avoids eye contact. Although the food is delicious, the bill is much more than Anthony intended to spend when he invited his girlfriend for dinner.

The evening winds down, the restaurant closes, and the girls go home, Anthony's girlfriend quietly apologizing to him as they say goodnight.

The doors are locked leaving a bunch of close North End friends hanging out at the bar. There's Frankie Dinisi, Eddie Grceo, aka 'the Greek,' Henry Sorentino, aka 'Duke', Josie Mazzarekka, aka Josie 'Jazz', Ruth Enrisha, aka 'Reesha', from Bobby LaBella's after hours place, and Anthony.

Inevitably the conversation turns to the rudeness of Anthony's girlfriend's girlfriend. Some defend her.

Frankie says, "Anthony brought her here as his guest. She opens the menu. She's entitled to order anything she wants. She wanted lobster. Tough."

"She's a fucking slut," says Ruth. "It's twice the price of the Chicken Marsalas that the girlfriend and Anthony ordered. Use your fucking head. You're a guest. Follow their lead. Okay, order veal. A buck or two more than what they ordered. But Christ, and then ordering that side that most people have as a main course...?"

"Yeah. She's a slut. That's how those Iraeshas all are. Ignorant," Reesha says.

"Still. She probably doesn't get to eat out much in nice restaurants. And her girlfriend didn't stop her," Frankie says.

"You're supposed to know," says Duke. "You're just supposed to know these things."

Outside, the snow is falling, but quietly, not interrupting the conversation that flowed continuously. Everyone wanted to be heard. By now it was 3.30am.

Frankie offered his own such experience.

"So it's 9.00, I'm sitting at the bar and two 'wiseguys' come in. So I want to buy them a drink."

Duke says, "Why did you want to buy them a drink?"

"Whaddya mean? I want to show respect."

Eddie the Greek says, "You're an asshole. You don't show them respect. You're not in their league. You're a fucking waiter. You work for a living. No one expects you to pay for them."

"Eyy. I'm not you. I respect people," Frankie says.

Anthony says, "Alright. What happened?"

Frankie pauses.

"Ha!" the Duke says. "They told you to mind your own fucking business."

Frankie shook his head and, his voice now lacking confidence, says, "They each ordered a bottle of Taittinger, 1973, the best on the wine list."

Everyone at the table laughed and jeered. "Why are you laughing?" Frankie says. "I was being a nice guy. That wasn't right."

"You were being a jerk. And they're connected. You don't have the right to force them to say thank you. You don't even know them," says the Duke.

"I don't have that right? I didn't know."

"You're supposed to know," Anthony says.

By 4.00am the gang breaks up. Everyone lives in the North End except Frankie, and he has no way of getting home. Anthony is stuck and invites Frankie to sleep over at his house.

"But be quiet coming in. I live with my parents, my aunt, and my sister and my brother." The pair get to the apartment, go into Anthony's room, and instantly fall asleep.

It's 9.00am when Anthony gets out of bed and walks into the kitchen. The apartment is well-lit from the reflection off the snow that continues to blanket the universe outside. All of Anthony's family is around the table, waiting for the second pot of coffee to finish percolating.

"Anthony," his sister says, "What a racket last night. That snoring kept me up all night. I'm dying to meet this girl of yours, snoring like that. She must be something else."

Anthony sits but says nothing. Then the door to Anthony's room opens and out comes Frankie Gavo, still dressed in his tuxedo. Although everyone knows each other, the anomaly of Frankie in tuxedo, in the morning, in their apartment while they're sitting lazily around the table induces a silence that no one strives to break. Frankie takes a look around and spots the coffee pot. He walks over, picks up the pot, and proceeds to fill everyone's cup. Anthony finds an extra chair and Frankie sits, looking into his mug.

Finally, Anthony's sister speaks up. "How did you end up here?"

Frankie explains.

"But why didn't you go straight home after work? That early, you would have made it."

"I didn't know it was going to be this bad," Frankie says.

She replies, "You're supposed to know."

187

# North End Neighbors
## By Lino Viola

I came to the United States when I was not yet nine and my widowed mom and I went to live with her uncle in Medford. I do not know exactly what happened, but my mom had to leave for health reasons, and we moved to the North End. The year was 1956 that found me trying to transition from a two-family house in the suburbs to a cold water flat on the fourth floor at 161 Endicott Street. The Caruso's owned the building. Mr. and Mrs. Caruso had three children, two boys and a girl. Mr. Caruso was a lawyer and I remember seeing him faithfully, the first of each month as he would come knocking to collect the monthly rent of $28 for the three rooms and small bathroom which was inside the apartment unlike others that were outside and had to be shared by two families.

We left the Medford residence with our personal belongings only. My mom had to start to furnish the apartment from scratch. I remember the first night eating on the floor for we had yet to get a table. I remember that we purchased a used refrigerator that was missing the panel that covered the area on the bottom where the motor was. I remember the motor rested on two two by fours and occasionally I would see it spark when it kicked on and never suspected that a month or so later that it would be the source of a fire that engulfed the apartment.

It was around midnight when I heard and felt my mom frantically tugging at me to get up. I thought that she was joking when she said that there was a fire. The refrigerator sat between the two windows that overlooked the back of an enclosed courtyard. On the opposite side you could see the back of a building which fronted North Margin Street not far from the infamous Pizza Regina. Around each of the windows were sheer curtains that had already gone up in flames, flames that had now caught on to the frame of the bedroom door; flames that we foolishly would go through instead of using the fire escape; flames that were being fed by the linoleum flooring.

I remember standing in front of 154 Endicott St. in my pajamas looking up watching the firemen doing their best to put out the fire. It did not take long to put it out since we did not have a heck of a lot. The main damage was to the kitchen and thankfully the bedrooms were not touched. When all was said and done, we were told to stay out of the apartment for at least a week, the time needed to clear the air of the gaseous odors and smoke. Where do you go when you have no relatives? Going back to Medford was out of the question since my mom's uncle had taken ill.

This is where the true story of what the North End meant to me really starts. Without batting an eyelash, Mrs. C. who lived on the second floor offered to take me in for whatever time was needed to clean up the apartment - I had on occasion baby sat her two boys and they were all excited that I would be with them. At the same time the landlady had made a similar offer to my mom.

Even though we had no one, these two families stepped up alleviating the fears of where we would eat and sleep. Thanks to them my mom was able to continue to go to work and I did not miss a beat in school. Each night would find us on separate floors eating supper with people who just a month earlier were total strangers. People who did not have much space to share but made some for us.These two families were a microcosm of what the rest of this one square mile area was all about. People helping people.

Inside those cold facades of various colored bricks were some of the warmest and caring people on earth. It was the people that made the North End the special place that it was and will always be in my heart.

# Five Random Memories
## By Anthony Cintolo

*Responses to Random Memories*

*by Dom Capossela*

**- BROTHER GERARD chasing kids in No Bennet playground to go serve mass**

That's a memory. Brother Gerard was in charge of getting enough altar boys and other servers to assist the priests. Although he had many volunteers, there were never enough. Occasionally, the good Brother would come into the playground and physically grab a couple of the kids who reacted too slowly. The rest of us ran for our lives, scattering like so many leaves in the autumn wind.

**-PLAYING ERRORS "Off the wall is out but the red is a home run"**

We used the side of a building that had safe play space around it. The team that was up hit the ball; the other team fielded it. The 'batter' held the ball in his hand and smashed it against the building. He could direct the ricochet and, if it was in play, he would run the bases while the fielders tried to throw him out. We used a pimple ball. They were expensive but so much fun.

**-WAXED BASEBALL CARDS using "holy" wax**

Holy wax. We were not afraid of anything, including God. We stole candles from the Church, (Remember, we were altar boys and had access), and dripped the wax over baseball cards. Then we lined up and competed. Using a backhand motion, we propelled the card to glide through the air. When it landed, aided by the holy wax, it slid along the sidewalk to the building façade. The card that was closest to the building won. Cards or money.

**- TAMARINDO  making it, serving it, drinking it**

Tamarindo is not a popular drink in Italy. So I'm not sure how it came about that Burden's Pharmacy on Hanover St. in the North End, not only sold cold Tamarindo drinks, but actually made the syrup on premises from the Tamarindo fruit pods. The syrup, with sugar, and soda water made a refreshing drink.

## 3-CARD POKER  on any available flat surface

We loved to play cards. From pennies when we were five or six, to nickels, knuckles, dimes, quarters, dollars.

For hours on end.

*The Eucharist has been a key theme in the depictions of the Last Supper in Christian art, as in this 16th-century Juan de Juanes painting, after Leonardo da Vinci's Last Supper. Stories involving the host abound.*

## Body of Christ
### By Ron Polcari

Being brought up Catholic, I was taught to believe that receiving the host at mass was actually receiving the body of Christ.

I was in grammar school at St. Anthony's and used to go to mass every Sunday at St. Leonard's Church where I would receive communion.

This one Sunday after receiving the host I went back to my pew and promptly sneezed into my hand. The remnants of the host still in my mouth was just blown onto my right hand. I didn't move or touch my hand throughout the rest of the service and when it was over, I rushed out of the church to the nearby rectory. I rang the doorbell. A priest came to the door. I nervously said "I have Jesus on my hand" and explained about my untimely sneeze.

He calmed me down saying it was ok and that I could wash my hand.

Whew!

## Newspaper Route
### By Dom Capossela

While I did odd things to make money when I was young, my first seriously producing job was offered to me out of anger and spite.

Newspapers were an important source of America's news in the 1950s. Boston had two dominant papers, the broadsheet Boston Globe, for intellectuals, and the tabloid Boston Record-American for us working stiffs. To gain a much-needed competitive edge, the Record American published a half-dozen editions throughout the day, including late afternoon and nighttime editions. In Boston's North End, a tightly-packed, entirely-Italian community, the multi-edition Record was the dominant newspaper, especially the late-afternoon edition which carried the racing handle from which the bookies took the day's number.

The number? The numbers racket. The daily number, a form of illegal gambling played mostly in poor and working-class neighborhoods in the United States, wherein a bettor attempted to pick three (or four, for the big money) digits to match those that will be posted later in the day. You couldn't place a bet after 3pm: the bookies had to hand their slips into the 'office'

*Waiting for the truck of newspapers to arrive, champing at the bit to get started.*

immediately after 3pm. The "number" was the last three digits of "the handle", the amount racetrack bettors placed on race day at a major racetrack, published in racing journals and major newspapers in New York. Sometime after three o'clock.

(Note that the numbers racket was so profitable and so in-grained in certain working-class neighborhoods that the government started its own Lottery. Where police work failed, the Lottery drove the numbers racket out of business, even though the government Lottery only paid out 600 on 1,000 spent, where the bookies had been paying out 720 per 1000.)

Many people had their papers delivered to their door by a legion of newspaper boys. In the North End the newsboys would buy a stack of papers at half the printed cost from one of two cigar stores on Hanover St., Martini's or Fiore's, tobacco stores that doubled as bookie shops. As a newspaper boy you bought either from one or the other. And you were marked as belonging to that store only.

The cigar stores didn't wait for delivery of the late afternoon

*Newsies often worked late.*

edition. The first store to have the afternoon edition always sold fifty extra copies to the inveterate gamblers waiting desperately to buy the paper to see if they had suddenly become rich. And the delivery boys from the winning cigar store got their bundles early and always randomly hawked ten more copies than their counterparts who had to wait for their store's late arriving papers.

So each store had a car at the Record American printing plant in downtown Boston waiting to grab the newspapers as they came off the presses. Every day those two cars would race through the Boston streets with their stacks of newspapers and the racing handle. On the days that Fiore drove for the papers, he would always win. He ignored warning signs like red lights and stop signs. A bad habit of his. I was a 'Martini' boy. Even when Fiore wasn't driving, we usually lost this race. Sucked.

As a sad aside, one day, in broad daylight, Fiore was shot and killed in his own store. He had been warned to stop running his late-night Barbu (a card game for skilled gamblers) unless he started 'kicking up to the office'. Unlike his luck which held

195

steady all those times he ran the lights, he ignored the warnings from the local crime family once too often.

In the North End, the newsboys carved out routes by soliciting tenement customers building by building, slowly growing profitable customer bases. They kept their customers happy by never failing to deliver as scheduled and collecting the full cost of the newspapers plus a tip weekly, on Fridays, payday.

Traditionally, the boys respected blocks already serviced by someone else. We were too young for territorial wars.

Patsy had developed one of the biggest and richest routes in the neighborhood. He kept a small book in his pocket listing every customer by address. The book also served as a ledger for collections and had space for any idiosyncrasies, like dogs or rats on premises. To these home deliveries, which took him from 4.00pm to 7.00pm, he appended a street walk from 8.00pm to 10.00pm. This beat took him through the Combat Zone surrounding Scollay Square, adjacent to the North End.

But to sell on the street at night your customers wanted the late edition of the Record American. So after the home deliveries Patsy had to return to the store and pick up a fresh stack of the night edition papers. Sometimes he would run home for a quick supper between shifts.

One day Patsy announced to the gang that he had gotten a terrific job and wanted to give up his newspaper route. Now Mario and Patsy had been best friends, the buildings they lived in were side-by-side. Mario should have inherited that route, but Mario's sister had rejected Patsy as a suitor and, in retaliation, Patsy rejected her whole family. Mario was not going to get that route. Mario offered to buy the route. No deal. Patsy wasn't giving Mario anything.

I was eight years old then, Patsy was twelve, and Mario was ten. Sometimes I had gone along Patsy's routes with him, helping to lug the huge stack of papers he carried in a large cloth bag that hung diagonally around his neck and across his chest. That sack freed both hands to pull out a newspaper, fold it in half, and one-hand it to the street-customer while receiving payment and tip with the other. At the end of the night Patsy would give me a dime for keeping him company. In the North End we were all poor. But among the poor, my family was dirt and that dime was the most money I had ever held in my hands.

One night, about a week before his retirement, he told me to come with him on his route. Ten cents! I spent it in my mind fifteen times. You could buy a lot for $1.50. I was excited. My excitement turned to stun when, as we walked out of Martini's with our stack of papers, Patsy handed me his book. I took it without understanding the meaning. "Where do we start?" he asked, using his chin to direct me to open the book. I read the name and address. "Well, let's go." And with that, Patsy handed the fortune-making route over to me. In the event, the customers couldn't care less.

Mario cared. I had deprived him of something he lusted over. Incensed, yes but more like furious. He threatened me. He was two years older, bigger, but less aggressive, less maniacal. I swung minutes before the thought would have entered his mind. But eventually it would have. Two punches: to his cheek bone and then to his ear and head. He fell back three steps before he stumbled into a bicycle and fell to the ground crying, in front of a crowd of Endicott St. locals who shook their heads and walked away, disappointed the fight didn't last longer.

The route proved to be crazily lucrative producing a huge amount of money. For the first week or two Patsy took tips that he had earned but not received in the days leading up to the transfer. Those tips barely dented the scads of bills I took home. Even after I paid out Patsy, I made a huge amount of money, like $25.00 a week, almost half of what my father earned.

Without her asking, I gave my mother $5.00 every week. She took it without looking at me. She just nodded. Once in a while my father gambled or drank some of his paycheck. Then my mother would ask if I could pay the oilman or the milk man. I always did. We were always at the outer credit limit of every purveyor. I really don't know how my mother coped. She was naturally a very nervous person. On Saturday mornings she and my father did our budget, choosing whom they wouldn't be able to pay this week. And she had to face these people day after day. Four kids. Three meals a day. And snacks. No spending money. Poor woman. Not the life my father had envisioned, either.

The worst thing about the job was that in the summer my arms got black from ink. And there was an element of loneliness: my friends were hanging out with each other, learning to roller skate and to build scooters out of orange crates and roller blades. On the other hand, I bought myself an endless stream of delicious hot fudge sundaes in the afternoons, and hot dogs late at night at a Scollay Square dump called the White Tower. They were delicious. Ten cents.

I enjoyed walking the streets of Scollay Square. I stayed on the main streets and walked slowly, listening to the most God-awful sounds of music from inside the bars. Once in a while the doors would open in such a way I could see women in underwear. They were mostly very homely and very old and tired. Drunks might wave me into the bar, take a newspaper and give me a big tip before the bouncer could reach me. "F--- you," I said when I reached the door.

It was during my newspaper sojourn that my father had the proudest moment in our lives together. One night I got picked up by some law enforcement person. He accompanied me home and gave my father a ticket that demanded he appear in Court. The state didn't like eight-year-olds walking Scollay Square at night hawking newspapers.

That man told the judge what he caught me doing. Who knew selling papers was a crime? The judge called my father to stand and explain himself.

My father was typically a fearful man. Not this day. He rose as well as he could, he carrying around a tree stump instead of a left leg. He spoke of our poverty. Of the real-crimes alternative to unusual work.

Of family. Of doing something admirable. Of the work ethic. Of still shining in school.

I had never seen my father like a lion before: growling, eating up the judge. I was prouder of my father then than I had ever been before or would ever be again.

"Go home," was all the judge said.

I learned many lessons selling newspapers but perhaps the biggest takeaway was honing the art of making deals. Not so much from the staid home deliveries, but the street-hawking, where every paper sold was an opportunity to make an outsized tip.

From my first day as a newsboy I was never again without money.

## An Ode to Bocce
### By Victor Passacantilli

Sunday mornings the US Constitution's cannon booms

Signaling 8 am

Lifelong boyhood friends gather in their beloved North End

To compete at bocce and revive an old-world pastime that

Their fathers and grandfathers played and they mocked as youngsters

A rite of passage for septuagenarian ancestors

Reliving the love and steadfastness of the game of bocce A tradition filled with the enduring fervor of competition and lots of friendly kibitzing!

*Bocce is a very popular activity among older North Enders*

## Jimmy Wasn't Thankful
### By Sammy Viscione

Jimmy, a Sheafe St. neighbor of mine who's profession was waitering, and who also excelled at consuming liquor, was a victim one stormy snowy nite while being inebriated. As he haphazardly ventured his way thru the storm after leaving the Lucerne bar in the West End, he was spotted by North End guys who forcibly placed him in their vehicle under physical and indistinguishable verbal protest by Jimmy. Knowing that he lived at #7 Sheafe St. they proceeded to drive him home. Well, a couple of weeks later Jimmy was approached by one of the guys and informed him that he was one who helped him to safely get home . Expecting a warm thank you, Jimmy told him, "You did me a favor? You guys helped me? You bastards. I was around the corner from my apartment in the West End when you drove me to Sheafe St. I moved from there a month

# St Anthony's Procession
## By Vince Amicangelo

St. Anthony's School, Columbus High, Boston College

Back when I was 9 or 10, my father sent me to pick up some papers from Pascali (Pat) DiMasi (Sal DiMasi's uncle). His office was in Gabe Piemonte's office and building on the corner of Hanover and Cross (Mother Anna's is there now). In that building also lived Bill Marlowe (Famous disc jockey, also the voice for Spiedel Watch Band, Cologne and FLoramos (Where the meat falls off the bone) and Ron Polcari (Rockin' Robin, also a famous dj).

While I was walking past Arthur's (Ist discount store in the North End) bouncing my pimple ball, it hit a crack and bounced into the street and into a '41 Cadillac limo, with its back door open (embarrassing door) this man picked it up and gave it to me.

I looked at him and said, "Hey, mister, I know you. You carried the banner at the "St. Anthony's Procession."* He smiled and said, "Thanks for remembering me," and tossed me a quarter.

I picked up my father's papers and ran straight to Fiore Cristy's where I bought a funny book, a bag of chips, and a coke. And by the way, that man's name was John F. Kennedy!

# We Knew Who We Were
## By Steve Paterna

All this magic imbued us with the knowledge that there is no other place.

Steve Paterno, a scoutmaster for five years at one of our Settlement Houses, reports this:

In his efforts to empower some of the North End residents to enhance the quality of our lives, John Dexter, Mr. D, would take me and four or five of my scouts for a three-day trip to his home in Vermont, trips that sometimes included an excursion into Montreal. On one such excursion, our waitress asked, "Where are you from?"

One of the scouts blurted out, "We're from the North End."

"Oh?" she said. "The North End of where?"

"Boston, of course. Where else? I thought everybody knew that."

"Well," she said, "That must be quite a place."

He answered, "Of course! Best place to live. It's great."

Mr. D leaned over to me and said softly, "Now you know why I adopted the North End as my home."

Why, indeed. You grow up in that place at that time and, in truth, there is no other place.

# An Early North End Memory
## by Alex Goldfeld

I first moved to the North End in 2001, a little more than a year after getting married. We found a little apartment on Salem Street, a few doors up from Prince. Even though I am from a small, rural town in Connecticut, I had always been drawn to Boston's North End. While it would take years for Mariel and me to learn many of the unique stories and traditions of this neighborhood, we quickly discovered that we shared the same values: family, hard work, and respect for one's community.

These values became clear when the rowdy, student-filled apartments on Prince Street were keeping us awake late into the night. There was a collection of trees inside our block, bounded by Salem, Prince, Margaret, and Sheafe Streets. Make a lot of noise in your apartment, especially on the Prince Street side, and we could all hear it through the trees in the big rectangle of buildings. My neighbor next door on Salem, a middle-aged North Ender, took me with her a few times on midnight raids into the Prince Street parties. We insisted folks close their back windows, turn down their music, and wrap up the parties. Most of the young people were shocked at our presence and demands, and they were definitely more scared of my neighbor than they were of me. We made no threats, but we sternly taught them that they needed to respect those around them.

In 2003, Mariel and I moved around the corner to Tileston Street. We were fumbling with the keys at the front door on our first day, and a lady popped her head out of the fourth-floor window to ask who we were and why we were there. Once we identified ourselves, she came down and let us in. Later that evening, her older sister came down from the second floor with some of her macaroni and gravy. Their grandfather had built the building almost one hundred years earlier, and they welcomed us into their home as we made our own on the first floor.

Back then, more than twenty years ago, Salem Street was still filled with small shops, and we got everything we needed at D & R Meat Market, Polcari's, Martignetti's, Dairy Fresh Candies, the True Value, and Bova's ... not to mention haircuts, video rentals, produce at the Haymarket, and even the occasional coffee at the Dunkin at 66 Salem. Importantly, these were places frequented by our neighbors and were mostly run by people from North End families, even if they didn't live in the neighborhood. I learned a lot about the culture of this little district, still separated from the rest of town by the Central Artery, by talking with the elder Mr. Rothman at the back of the hardware store; or with Danny as he bagged up my favorite chocolate-covered blueberries at Dairy Fresh; or even while playing foosball at the Different Drummer.

The North End at the dawn of the twenty-first century was still a small town where you could, even as outsiders like us, get to know just about everyone. Well, perhaps not every one, but it did feel that way. I went on to work in the North End for two decades, including writing and lecturing about the area, and leading "Tours with Alex." I co-founded the North End Historical Society to share and preserve everything I had learned about the neighborhood I love. But the first thing I recall about settling on these storied streets are the Italian American Bostonians who took a chance on a Jewish kid from Connecticut and welcomed me into their extended family.

# A North End Story:
## Growing Up on the Best Block in the North End
### By Victor Passacantilli

I was born on September 8, 1943, the day Italy surrendered to the Allied Forces during World War II. My maternal grandmother, Anna Grasso suggested to my parents that I be named in commemoration of the King of Italy Vittorio Emmanuel III. My parents settled on Victor.

I was taken home to 4 Fountain Place on Hanover Street and lived there until I was 4 or 5 when we moved to 422 Hanover Street on top of the Blue Front Restaurant. I remained at that address until June 20th 1965 when I got married and moved to Medford.

I can readily recall how fortunate I felt as a youngster to be living on a linear 100 yard block of Hanover Street stretching from Charter Street to the corner of Commercial Street.

In my estimation it was the best "corner" in the North End to grow up on. On that stretch of North End real estate I had my entire family at one time. My parents, 4 grandparents, 5 brothers, 3 uncles, 3 aunts, 10 cousins and a great aunt and uncle. Also, that block was teeming with many boy and girl friends my age.

If you spanned the block to the corner of Clark Street you'd find an entire Italo-American village where one could conceivably be born, reside, get married, raise a family, earn a living, socialize in a club, enjoy fine dining, hang out, meet friends and play cards in a bar room, get a haircut, use a women's hair salon, play a number, bet a horse, dog or game, have a house call by a doctor, fill a prescription, play errors off the base of an historical statue, play "buck buck how many fingers up," play hide and seek where the hiding places were under cars, in doorways and in cellars, spin tops in the middle of the street, ride home made scooters on the sidewalks, attend mass and receive the sacraments, have your clothes altered and dry cleaned, buy Italian bread, cookies and a slice of pizza, buy groceries and produce, buy freshly cut meat and poultry, buy penny candy, patronize 2 coffee shops, fill your car with gas and have it serviced, attend a protestant church, visit 3 saint chapels, play pool, use a travel agency, patronize a hardware store and when it all came to an end, you could be waked in a funeral parlor... all that without venturing out beyond Clark Street or *having to turn on to another street.* And in the event of a catastrophe, the Fire House was on the block and the US Coast Guard Base was there at the end of Hanover Street to protect us from any foreign invasion by sea!

To my *"Americani"* friends and colleagues I have often recounted that growing up in the North End was like living on an island. On the island everyone dressed like me, ate like me, talked and acted like me. We shared so many similar experiences on the streets, corners and playing fields in our North End. What an incredible neighborhood wherein most of us had the cherished opportunity to be a part of. An ethnic enclave beloved by us and surely envied by others!

# My Memory of the Old North Church Steeple Disaster
## By Nick Di Masi

Growing up as a little boy, our apartment was located right next door to the famous Old North Church in Boston's North End. We lived on the third floor of a four-story building and the windows in our breakfast and dining rooms looked right out to the church. I can remember every morning almost in the shadow of the steeple on the church and looking at that steeple with admiration. It was a beautiful steeple to a beautiful church.

Well, the year was 1954. It was early September and we heard on the news that a hurricane was heading our way, namely Hurricane Carol. School was cancelled that day due to the hurricane and I sat by the window of our apartment watching the wind pick up outside. All of a sudden, I began to notice that the steeple was swaying in the wind. I screamed to my mother that the steeple was going to fall. She came to the window and assured me that the steeple would not fall, and she tried to calm me. I said to my mother, ''mom the wind is blowing east to west, but if it changes directions, the steeple will fall directly on our apartment." She tried to assure me that everything would be alright, but it didn't work. I was scared. After about an hour, a policeman came loudly knocking on our door. We were instructed to abandon our apartment in case the wind shifted. My mother gathered all three of us boys and we all rushed in the wind and rain to walk down to our cousin's apartment which was the next street over. Just before we left, my mother had called my father at work to tell him about the problem and asked him to move his car because it was parked in a spot on the street where the steeple would crash on top of it.

When we got to my cousin's apartment, the curiosity of a twelve-year-old boy like me could not be contained, and I told my mother that I was going to watch the steeple fall. She was reluctant to let me go, but she could not stop me as I ran out the door. When I got to where we lived, I could see my father arguing with the police officers because, by this time, the police had cordoned off the area and were not going to allow my father to get to his car. Well, I stood there in amazement as I watched the steeple fall. I heard it and I saw the wood pretty much bury my father's car. It was a memory of a disaster that I experienced as a child and will never forget. We were so lucky that the wind did not change direction and destroy our home at the time. The next day, I remember seeing a picture on the front page of the newspaper showing the steeple on top of my father's car. It was and is my most vivid child's memory moment!

## The Reunion
### By Nick Di Masi

Once a year since 1972 I have attended the Friends of the North End annual reunion. This is a group founded in 1972 and consists of all the young boys who grew up in the North End in the 1940s and 1950s in a very small section of Boston called the North End. We were all second and third generation Americans of Italian immigrants who came to the US in the early part of the 20th century.

Now, what is amazing about this reunion is that, after all these years, we still get 250 men to attend this reunion. How many neighborhoods the size of one square mile can get that many men to return to a reunion of friends that they had as young boys growing up?

During the 1950s this neighborhood was considered one of the most congested neighborhoods in the whole of America. There were many families all stacked into apartments in four story apartment tenement houses that would be considered substandard today, mainly because many of them were ''cold water" flats without central heat and no showers or baths. Can you imagine having to go the local bathhouse for your daily or weekly shower? Well, all we boys did that. Despite these inconveniences, we were all mostly happy boys. We played sports and various games just like other boys our age, even though we had concrete playgrounds in the neighborhood. We all went to schools and had forty or fifty kids in each class. Can you imagine that today? We all walked to school. We walked to church. We walked to all the stores we needed. One of my friends said that we were the only neighborhood that had twelve bakeries, three hardware stores, seven churches, three laundromats, ten barber shops seven dry cleaners, one chicken slaughter shop and five butcher shops. We were self-sufficient.

Every kid in the neighborhood had a nickname and we still call them by their nicknames when we meet at the reunion. It is a wonderful time, and as I leave the reunion, I sometimes think what a wonderful country we live in because almost all of us have turned out to be good citizens and have assimilated into American society quite well. Some of you may even have met us in your work or in your social contacts here in the suburbs where most of us live now. It is a nice feeling to get back with childhood friends, and we hope to keep this group going for a long, long time.


## Fistfights, But No Weapons
### By Lino Viola


To my best recollection this occurred during the summer of 1960. I was thirteen years old and working my first job selling newspapers for a Jewish man, who I knew as "Curley." He manned the newsstand at the entrance of the Union Street Station, and I worked at his other stand at the rotary which housed the entrance to Haymarket Station prior to it being torn down by the BRA. It was a busy spot with lots of traffic. I had just finished giving directions to a couple of tourists who were looking for Durgin Park Restaurant when suddenly I felt a sharp object in my back and someone telling me to give them the money I had in my apron. I gave them all my change and the few dollars I had and with that they ran off. I did get a glimpse of them but did not recognize them. I immediately ran down to Union Station to tell my boss who contacted the police.

A detective came, asked me some questions, and left. I soon ended my day and walked a few blocks home which was at the end of Cooper Street. I had supper with my mom but did not trouble her with what happened. I figured she had enough on her plate being a widow and working in a sweat shop all day.

After supper I walked up the street to meet my friends from the Clinic and proceeded to tell them what happened earlier. They were concerned and asked a number of questions. As I gave them a description of the two boys, I saw running away, someone said, "I think I know who they are."

About eighteen of us walked to Sly Park. As we entered, I spotted the two boys at the far end, they were closed in, trapped and nowhere to run. They seemed to be frightened seeing our group approaching. One of my friends turned to me and asked if they were the ones. When I said yes, the two boys immediately started to apologize saying, "We didn't know he was a North End kid."

# The Feast Of All Feasts
## By Lucille Bova Guzzone

By 1890 the citizens of Boston's North End were nearly 99% Italian, and the area became " Little Italy " Italian culture permeated the area swiftly and completely. Their Catholic faith was the focus of their lives. They brought with them the traditions of Italy including celebrations and colorful feasts, and the honoring of their patron saint. These massive events still exist today.

Statues of the Saints laden in gold and money, are paraded throughput the neighborhood. Bands played , souvenirs and holy objects are sold in kiosks which are set up along the streets. The delicious food , including pizza, sausage, peppers, and delicacies permeate the air. In 1919 a precious statue of Saint Anthony was brought over from Montefalcione, a small town west of Naples. At the time, the Boston parish looked for a safe place to store the statue until the last weekend in August when the Saint would be brought out to be celebrated.

My grandmother's sister, aunt Rose Piccone lived in a large apartment located at 105 North Washington st. It had a living room perfectly suited for a makeshift chapel, a perfect home for the Saint. It remained there until circa 1958 when she passed away. As a child, I never really understood the significance of being so close to this piece of art.

Once a year, for about ten years, my cousin Johanne Brogna and I were dressed in brown robes, looking like miniature Franciscans , and marched in the parade along side the statue.

Recently I brought my daughter, daughter in law, and grandson to experience the feast. They were truly impressed when the parade passed by my aunts former home. There the men lowered the Saint in front of the door to honor her part in this historical event. What an amazing and tender moment for me and my family!

The National Geographic magazine once stated that this Feast of St. Anthony in Boston's historical North End was considered quote; "the Feast of all Feasts".

# Why Does It Take An Hour To Buy A Box Of Macaroni From A Store Just Five Minutes Away?
## By Dom Capossela

In our bustling neighborhood, where the streets teemed with life and energy, all the stores, and we have dozens, are close together.

On this day, Mama Olga is cooking and realizes she needs a box of rigatoni. Her husband had mentioned that they haven't had that pasta in a while. She puts down her implements, takes off her apron, and heads out to get the pasta, the round trip to take fifteen minutes. It is only 3.30pm: plenty of time to get back and start 5.00pm dinner.

Olga steps outside for the first time today. She's been washing the common hallway and stairs and her deep breath is pleasantly free of ammonia.

"Olga!" It's Linda Ferrara from across the street. Olga and Linda are best friends. Their children, they each have four, are best friends. Olga smiles and they hold hands. Linda says, "Olga, you'll never guess." "What," Olga says. "My Linda is going to become a nun." "Oh! How wonderful," Olga says, and the two are off on a ten-minute impromptu visit, followed by a five-minute gotta-hurry-goodbye.

Linda goes home, and Olga takes another dozen steps. "Oh, Olga!" It's Clara Sarno from Endicott St, a friend. "Hey, Clara. You look so good. How was the operation?" "It went fine," and the two talk for five minutes. They say goodbye for three more.

Olga crosses North Margin Street, a line already forming outside the Regina Pizzeria where you can buy a small cheese for .35 cents. She reaches the sidewalk and has to step aside to let LouLou turn the corner. LouLou is pushing a stroller. "Oh, LouLou. You had your baby?" Olga walks around the stroller and peers in. The baby is fast asleep. LouLou is beaming and for five minutes the two women talk baby talk: she's a restless sleeper but a good eater, her pee and poops are just fine. Then it's time to say goodbye, and another three minutes elapse.

And so it goes. She meets Auntie Mary, her sister-in-law, who just bought a couch, and they're delivering it today. Some other small talk, a three-minute goodbye, and then she meets Auntie Marie, a regular nighttime visitor, who'll be over tonight after supper. "No, no, I'm going to eat with my mother. After supper," Marie says. "What are you making?...Oh! Well, I'll always have a meatball." Olga's brother Dom, aka Blondie, is walking past. "Blondie, I thought you were in jail." "Yeah, but Frank Dimento showed up and got me released. They got nothing on me." "That's a good thing," Olga says. This goodbye is a perfunctory fifteen seconds, Blondie always has to see a man about a horse. Here comes her grandson, reluctantly crossing the street to say hello. He has a black eye and the last thing he wants to talk about is how he got it. It's the only thing Olga wants to talk about.

Olga reaches the store and picks out her pasta. Another customer asks what she is making? "I don't like Gravy the second night," she offers, like Olga does. Ha! She serves it because it's cheap. Then the customer says, "Olga, my daughter's getting married," and Olga interrupts for details on the groom and when and the size wedding. When Olga finishes with her questions, the customer asks, "Do you know of any apartments coming empty? My daughter needs a place to live. We don't want her to move to Everett or some other place that's dangerous." "Yeah, maybe," Olga answers. "Tell her to go the DiPrizio's lunch place on Endicott Street. Their grandfather just died this morning, suddenly, and he had a nice apartment." It doesn't matter that grandpa is still lying on the bed in the bedroom. North End apartments were rarely available, and the parents have to get down to business. The conversation zeroes in on the number of rooms, the windows, the light, and how much they were asking. "$28.00, but you better pay the first of the month. They're funny that way." "Alright, thank you so much, Olga. I'll go right now, when I finish my shopping."

On the return trip, Olga stops for just a minute each with Zizzy DeLuca and Yvonne DiCarlo, those minutes plus three minutes each to say goodbye. By the time Olga gets home with her box of rigatoni, it's 4.30pm and she needs to sit and have a cup of coffee. Then she starts the pot of water for the pasta. Dinner's is going to be late. Just a few minutes.

## Our Mother's Magic
### By Johanne Brogna

After spending hours scouring the market procuring the best of meats, fish, vegetables and fruits for affordable prices then laboriously lugging them up many tenement flights of stairs, our mothers would concoct a sumptuous meal expeditiously. I rarely witnessed, but marveled.

How they would prepare gravy, macaroni while baking or frying meats or fish beside preparing vegetables and salad. Their deft handling various sizes of pots, pans and utensils simultaneously was amazing. And meals were rarely tardy. Cooking for holidays and special occasions were their all-star game. Albeit a dieter's nightmare. Solely, and despite their age, wellbeing and an active Nonna they consistently produced an Ambrosia with God's blessing. this labor of love was a true unheralded testimony for the love they possessed for their loved ones. Over the years I attempted to but could not emulate them. And now, as in the years gone by, I feel from the heart of my heart I am glad I couldn't because when I give thought to the tireless efforts, culinary skills, and devotion it provokes the memory of my mother which embraces my heart and soul.

Grazia Mama. Per sempre nel mio cuore.

## The Games We Played
### By Nick Di Masi

Every now and then, I will think back to when I was a child growing up in the rather narrow streets of Boston's North End and the games we used to play on those streets. When I watch my grandchildren play today, it is hard for to relate because they are, more often than not, playing organized sports,* (with elaborate leagues like their almost professionally oriented basketball league, or their baseball endeavors on beautifully landscaped fields for Little League Baseball).*

Today, I thought I would write about some of the games I played. You may not be able to relate to these games because, quite frankly, in the North End of Boston, unlike today, there were no fields on which to play. We played on asphalt playgrounds or on streets with curbs. So, here are some games.

The first one was called "Scatter." This was a simple game of someone *blinding his eyes and counting to ten as we all ran and hid. He would then go looking for each of us and when he found one of us, he would bring him to the "goo" or jail. If one of us who was free ran into the "goo," we would holler " Relievio" and all the guys in the "goo" were set free. The game ended when all the participants were caught and put in the "goo."

The second game was called "Buck Buck How Many Fingers

Up." There were two teams. One guy would stand against the wall of a building, and all of his teammates would bend from the waist down, and hold the boy in front of him around the waist. So, you would have five or six guys form a flat surface with their backs. Then each guy on the other team would leap onto the flat surface one by one and wrap his legs around the waist of the boy bent over. If our weight collapsed the flat backs of the other boys, we won. If all managed to get on the surface, then our leader would holler "Buck Buck How Many Fingers Up" while holding a number of fingers up. If the leader of the other team guessed right, then we were the losers and had to form another flat surface with our bodies.

We would always try to imitate a baseball game. First we would take an old broomstick and a rubber pimple ball and play a game called "Stickball," often times in the narrow streets with the buildings closing in on us, not like on the asphalt playground. Needless to say, you had to hit the ball straight to get a hit.

Another way of imitating baseball was to take the pimple ball and throw it against the side of a building the had a point on the concrete and then run the bases as the ball flew out. This game was called "Errors." Believe it or not, I never owned a leather baseball glove, so I never played real baseball.

The third way to imitate baseball was to go onto one of asphalt playground fields and play "Punch Ball." We used the pimple ball. We would make our hand into a fist and try to punch the ball as far as we could, while we ran the bases.

A game we played when I was very young was called ''Time.'' All participants would sit in a row, while two other boys went off to pick a time. Then we each tried to guess what time it was. If you guessed right, then the two children who were hiding the time had to guess your favorite ice cream flavor or something like that. Whoever got it right, became your partner in the game, and you two went off to pick a time.

Another game was called "Pitch." In this game you pitched Topps Baseball Cards against the side of a building and tried to get the cards to stand on end against the  side of the building.

We also played a game called "Kick the Can," where we kicked a can down the street and then went to hide before the player who was "it" retrieved the can and came to look for you.

At the indoor settlement houses, we played a lot of ping pong and lot of board games like checkers and chess. I am happy that those games are still around. One of my great joys was teaching my grandchildren to play chess.

We never played "Jump Rope or Hopscotch." Those were considered girl's games when I was a kid.

My family could not afford a scooter for me, so I built my own scooter by getting a piece of lumber and attaching the split ends of our roller skates to each end of the board, while an old wooden fruit box acted as our handles to hold onto as I rode our improvised scooter. I never owned a bike. There was no place to store it, and my dad could not afford it. We were pretty poor.

All in all, it was a very happy childhood with a lot of games using whatever was available to us. It is amazing how happy one could be when you are little and don't have much money, but are determined to have fun.

# Violence Within
## By Dom Capossela

How was it that with so many young, testosterone-laden men crowding close, we never had a gang fight? And why did our daily fisticuffs never escalate into the use of knives or other weapons, and, contrarily, invariably ended with a handshake and, sometimes, even a hug?

The total absence of gang fights and the strict rules governing individual fistfights testified to the neighborhood's underlying social and cultural norms: the Italian heritage, close friendships, and blood ties. And to that we were of the same generation, sharing music, school, church, loves and hatreds, sports, activities, and gang codes, all feeding our identities and camaraderie; and, of course, we were all from the North End, the self-contained, parochial aspects of ghetto-life accentuating our commitment to the neighborhood's collective well-being against the outside world.

"No. no!" That deep voice came from Phillip, a respected corner guy, tough, twenty-something. We didn't know for sure if he was connected, but, at the least, he fit in with the office and, so, among us, his word was law. "That's not how we do things here. Put that away. Save it for outsiders. If you guys want to fight, let's go behind the school." Someone tucked the bat in a corner where it would be safe in plain view.

It was Valentine's Day and, on that day, the nuns let us give one single valentine to whomever we chose. Although all the girls' hearts were fluttering, the pretty girls got cards by the handfuls; the plainer girls, not so many. We were twelve years old.

Tony liked Rosalie, who didn't? She had a bright smile and was charming. Now in the sixth grade, her figure was well-developed and drew the desires of the boys, the jealousy of the girls. Despite rumors that she had a boyfriend, Tony overcame his nerves and excitement and handed her an envelope, insisting she open it then, despite the gang of kids the gesture drew. This could be trouble.

She gently tore the envelope and pulled out the card. It was a cartoon-bear declaring, "I love you 'beary' much". She smiled at Tony and, almost silently, said, "Thank you."

Why was Rosalie so quiet? Because she had, just two days ago, agreed with Giusto, asking on George's behalf, to be George's girlfriend. And so today, George, on the periphery of the group surrounding, took umbrage at Tony's audacity.

Nothing more to be said between Tony and Rosalie, the group broke up, heading to their classes. George pushed his way through the waves of students until he got next to Tony, and, in a low voice, said to him, "As soon as school is over, I'm gonna wait outside the building and break your fucking head." To which Tony, like George, one of the bigger, more physical schoolboys, responded, "Fuck you, asshole. She took my card. She likes me. We'll see who gets her after school." Friends of the two sidled up to each to lend support by clenching fists and glaring at the other side.

School ended and, with Phillip leading the way, forty kids, boys and girls both, walked, unobtrusively, we thought, to the rear of the school building to a space hidden from casual view. Tony and George took off their winter coats, handing them to their informal seconds. Some of the kids shouted encouragement to one or another of the combatants, some smiled giddily. Most were somber.

Once everyone was inside the enclosed space, Phillip waved the combatants over to himself and put a hand on the shoulders of each of the boys. First he said to the crowd, "Hey, back up. You're too close." We all did what we were told. Then to the adversaries he said, "This is over when one of you quits. And I mean then it's over. Got me?" The boys nodded unsterstanding. Phillip released them and stepped away from them saying, "Go for it."

There was some taunting, some encouragement from the on-lookers, but mostly, they were quiet. The reality was sinking in: someone they knew and cared for was about to be hurt. The faces of the fighters threatened a determination to punish their opponent.

Their hands went up in the traditional boxer's ready position and, absent a preconceived strategic fight plan, they immediately closed to each other, leaning left and right from the waist looking for a tactical advantage. Tony struck first, rotating his hips and torso and bending his elbow. Thrown in a sweeping arc, the hook was powerful and fast, and struck George's nose, blood instantly gushing from the break.

To his gang, George was to say afterwards, "When that first punch landed, I didn't feel a thing. But then I could only see him. My enemy. I didn't hear anyone else, didn't see anyone else. I had to shake my head, I was a little dizzy. Like close to being knocked out."

Two years ago, the sight of so much blood would have immediately ended the fight. But we were growing up fast. Leadership positions and Rosalie might be among the prizes hinging on the outcome of this match. George stumbled back three or four steps, and Tony didn't pursue. A mistake, ceding the momentum to his opponent.

220

George rebounded from the blow and sprang to the attack, unleashing a series of half a dozen strikes to Tony's head, ears, cheeks, and arms. Tony stumbled back, tripped over his own feet, and fell to the concrete. His lip was split and blood was coming out of his mouth.

To his gang, Tony was to say afterwards, "I was tasting my own blood. Metallic. For some reason, that's when I really decided to hurt that bastard. Tasting my blood was like tasting victory."

Although it took a long moment for Tony to regain his balance, George did not press his advantage. The two wounded warriors, rubbing their eyes, faced each other again in the ready-position, stepping around each other, regaining some energy. Bodies swaying, feet positioning, the taste of blood mixing with the salt of sweat and the viscosity of spit, for each, anger and hate were mixed with a newfound respect. Their adrenaline surges were tempered with caution. Had either of them the opportunity to call off the fight...but neither could, not without being labeled 'chicken'.

Quiet settled on the onlookers. This was for real. Injury and pain were being meted out. The attacks were neither easy to absorb nor pretty to watch. Some of the girls were crying. Even battle-tested Phillip was uncomfortable.

Breaking the stalemate, Tony leaped first, his lightning-quick strokes knocking George backwards. The sound of his bare fists connecting with flesh echoed through the hidden playground, bringing fear, sorrow, and even terror to us non-combatants. We were too young to provide our own law and order, our own referee to call the fight over. A draw. No one would ever, ever call the police. But who'll stop the rain?

George regained his balance and, when Tony paused his attack, George charged into Tony, grabbing him in a headlock with his left arm, his right fist piston-pounding repeatedly into Tony's face. The thud, thud, thud of contact made Tony dizzy, nauseous. But, by repeatedly punching George in the ribs and belly, he finally broke free and the fighters parted.

221

Never give an inch. Blood was dripping from both their faces, one eye of each was closed, and their knuckles were bleeding. But the two squared off at each other yet again, in a waltz of strategy and instinct, determination and inevitability. In two minutes, only one would be standing, triumphant.

Phillip, part of the crowd, looked at the bruised and battered faces of the two boys, exhausted fighters pushed to their limits, continuing their fight with sheer willpower. Could he allow this to continue? Look their parents in the eyes and say, "They had to fight it out?"

Impulsively, he stepped forward between the wounded warriors, his arms extended to keep them apart. "Come here," he ordered. The two dropped their hands and quietly obeyed. They knew it was over. Both were relieved. He returned his hands to their shoulders. Looking back and forth, from one to the other, "We're done here," he said. Neither responded. Each glanced from his opponent to the ground and back to the other's face. Phillip shook their shoulders.

"We're done here," he repeated. "Agreed?" The two stared at each other, reluctantly nodded at first, and then nodded with conviction. "Shake hands," he ordered. They did. They looked at each other. Respect blossomed, and in a flash, their arms were around each other's necks, pulling their heads together, pressing. They were close to tears.

A moment later they each slowly returned to their inner circles. The fight over, the pugilists led the ensemble out from the rear of the building. All emotion was drained. There was little conversation.

I don't remember if Rosalie stayed for the fight, nor which of the boys was her boyfriend the next day, if either. I do know those two never fought each other again, and, if thereafter they weren't best friends, they were friendly, even, on occasion, sticking up for each other.

# Each Picture Worth a Thousand...

*Words words words*
*I'm so sick of words*
*I read words all day through*
*First from him now from you.*
*Is that all you blighters can do?*

Let's take a peek at some great photos,
keeping our remarks to a minimum.

*He was yelling that his pizzas were Hot! Hot! In dialect he'd*
*be saying, "Cowoda, cowoda!". How proud Italians were to*
*be working, especially dispensing delicious food.*

*The crammed blend of street vendors and store fronts c1945 at Cross St. with Victor Minghella the one-man band. Do you believe in magic?*

*Many North Enders worked the fishing boats. Hours were unusual and the work was exhausting, but they loved the life.*

*This is how many women cleaned the outside of their windows. Whenever my mother sat on the window ledge to wash the windows, most of her body cantilevered over the cement sidewalk three flights below, my heart pounded with fear.*

*We grew up safely on the streets with each other, starting at age three. We grew up tight and protective.*

*We needed to cooperate with each other to install one end of our clotheslines on each other's property.*

*How proud was Ralph Polcari in his coffee store? Look at how neat and rich it was. Say no more.*

*I loved Cherrystone off the pushcart. My mouth watered when I passed by. But who could afford them? When I did have the quarter, I was at the pushcart for three of them. I loved the sound of the knife scraping against the shell. Loved the smell of lemons and tobacco sauce. And loved, loved, loved the smell and taste of the salt water and the feel of the clams, still alive, perhaps, as I sucked those babies down.*

*The handsome guy on the far left, my cousin Bobby, died prematurely.*

*Remember the motorcycle gang crashing
the bar in De Niro's "The Bronx Tale"?
They could have filmed that sequence
here.*

*At their height, local societies took turns sponsoring a weekly street festival. They were exciting adds to the already festive 'school's out' jubilation of our 2500-strong grammar school population. Normal bedtimes were suspended so the celebration went on.*

*The societies used the proceeds to pay for the costs of sponsoring a feast. The profits went to local charities.*

*We certainly did our share of posturing. But we weren't fakers. Underneath the tough guy veneer were tough guys. Violence was as integral a part of our personalities as going to Mass and Communion on Sundays.*

*Just hangin' out. What are you goin' to do tonight, Marty?*

*We started early on for pennies. As we got older, the stakes got higher.*

## Epilogue
### By Dom Capossela


The 1950s North End was a magical, once-in-a-lifetime neighborhood in which to grow up. Similar confined, energetic neighborhoods could be found elsewhere in America, but few, if any, with the cachet, the personality of us – *Urban Villagers, living in our Street Corner Society.*

We were buoyant, friendly, and exuberant people, confident of place and self, streetwise and people-smart, possessors of both an old-world understanding of the social value of small village life, and a spirit of youthful American optimism. We synergized and telescoped our communal tradition and energy into a palpable, vibrant warmth that penetrated visitors like a massage in a sauna, earning their oft-repeated return visits as well as their invitations for us to join in mainstream society.

We became these people by being always mindful of our separateness and our minority status; and we became these people by taking.
From our forebears, we inherited more than two millennia of artistic appreciation, sensitivity, passion, family values, vil-

238

lage-building skills, loyalty, and a hedonistic love of food, wine, and the opposite sex.

From our Roman Catholic schools and churches, we took discipline, respect, and a foundation in the values, knowledge, and beliefs of Western Civilization.

From our local American institutions, our library, bathhouse, and settlement houses, and the people who directed them, Mr. D, Mario, Ms. Herrick, Ms. Dennison, and others, we took our first glimpses of the world outside our tight borders.

Love and limitless sacrifice we took from our parents; loyalty and confidence from our friends.

From our country, the United States of America, we took respect for the rights of the individual.

From the thousands of visitors and tourists whose presence showed their appreciation of our neighborhood, we took a vindication of our odyssey, and an invitation to join middle-America, the big show.

We took, from within ourselves, the ability to assimilate and articulate these experiences.

And here, in our Little Italy, we blended these experiences, lessons, values, emotions, institutions, and freedoms, and we created the *Italo:* American born and raised, significantly influenced by Italian culture.

As payment for what we took, we gave a transformation of a hopeless 1900s slum into our own 1950s Emerald City, the metaphorical equivalent of our own personal development and growth in American society. We gave our North End, where the *gioia di vivere* of an Italian-rooted quotidian routine merged with the optimism that is America. We gave the 1950s North End: our quintessentially personal 'thank you'; our sociologically magical moment.